Wilbour J. Fay

The Didsbury Lectures, 1989

WISDOM IN THEOLOGY

The Didsbury Lectures

The Didsbury Lectures are delivered annually at the
British Isles Nazarene College, Manchester

Previous series are available as follows:

F. F. BRUCE, *Men and Movements in the Primitive Church*

I. H. MARSHALL, *Last Supper and Lord's Supper*

T. TORRANCE, *The Mediation of Christ*

J. ATKINSON, *Martin Luther: Prophet to the Church Catholic*

C. K. BARRETT, *Church, Ministry & Sacraments in the
    New Testament*

* D. GUTHRIE, *The Relevance of John's Apocalypse*

* C. E. GUNTON, *Christ and Creation*

Forthcoming:

J. D. G. DUNN, *Christian Liberty*

M. HOOKER, *The Death of Christ*

* These titles available from Eerdmans

WISDOM IN THEOLOGY

Ronald E. Clements

THE PATERNOSTER PRESS
CARLISLE

WILLIAM B. EERDMANS PUBLISHING COMPANY
GRAND RAPIDS, MICHIGAN

First published jointly 1992 by The Paternoster Press,
P.O. Box 300, Carlisle, Cumbria, CA3 0QS, UK,
and Wm. B. Eerdmans Publishing Co.,
255 Jefferson Ave. SE, Grand Rapids, Michigan 49503.

Printed in the United States of America

British Library Cataloguing in Publication Data

Clements, R.E.
Wisdom in Theology
I. Title
230'
Paternoster ISBN 0-85364-526-4

Eerdmans ISBN 0-8028-0576-0

Typeset by Photoprint, Torquay, Devon

Contents

Preface   7

Abbreviations   10

1.   Introduction   13

2.   Wisdom and the World   40

3.   Wisdom and Health   65

4.   Wisdom and Politics   94

5.   Wisdom and the Household   123

6.   Wisdom and the Divine Realm   151

Selected Bibliography   180

Index   182

Preface

The studies in the Israelite wisdom tradition presented here are based on the Didsbury Lectures given in the British Isles Nazarene College, Didsbury, Manchester in October 1989. Chapters 5 and 6 have been added to the original lectures in order to offer the reader a more comprehensive picture of the intellectual riches to be found in that tradition. Some of the material used in the original lectures was delivered in an earlier draft in The American Baptist Seminary of the West, Berkeley, California in April 1989. These were published as *Wisdom for a Changing World* (Bibal Press, Berkeley, 1990). All of this material has now been thoroughly revised and rewritten in the hope that the interpretations set forth here will be more fully integrated with other recent studies of the Israelite–Jewish wisdom tradition.

Having published a volume on Old Testament theology (1980) in which I took no account of the importance of the Israelite wisdom tradition, some redress for this omission was no doubt due. I am especially indebted for the stimulus to recognising the importance of this tradition provided by W. McKane, R. N. Whybray and J. L. Crenshaw all of whose friendship and interest in the subject have contributed much to my own concern with it. I should also wish to pay special tribute to the writings of Leo G. Perdue and R. L. Cohn whose writings have separately influenced very much the directions in which my thinking has moved.

On a practical level I am most grateful for the hospitality shown by the Faculty and students of both the American Baptist Seminary of the West, Berkeley, California and by that shown during my stay in the British Isles Nazarene College in Manchester. In view of the fact that I had originally hoped to have the material ready for the press by the time the original lectures were delivered, an apology is due for the delay in their final preparation. I hope, however, that, in view of the degree of interest currently displayed in the biblical wisdom tradition and the significant number of publications in the field, the delay may be excused. In company with many other students of the biblical tradition I am acutely aware of the complexity and importance which attaches to the growth of the Old Testament wisdom traditon. Both in regard to its roots in the earlier didactic literature of the ancient Near East, and the legacy which it bequeathed to both Jewish and Christian thought, its importance should not be under-rated. If we are able to establish such major intellectual constructions as a biblical world-view, and a biblical conception of virtue, then it would certainly appear that the wisdom tradition contributed greatly to both of these. That, at least, is part of the contention of these lectures.

It will be evident that for convenience I have grouped the major themes under various headings relating to aspects of daily life. It has become a commonplace to recognize that, while inheriting much from earlier traditions of didactic literature, especially that of Egypt, the Israelite wisdom teaching gave rise to ideas and concerns distinctive of its own context and origins. I have not been particularly concerned to trace features of uniqueness or commonality between the various traditions, since it is ultimately as a coherent whole that the material has been handed down to us.

I have endeavoured to provide a reasonable and helpful documentation to the extensive range of contemporary studies on the subject. In doing so, however, I sought to avoid unnecessary repetition and length since a number of excellent bibiographical essays on the topic are currently readily available.

I should especially extend my thanks to the Principal and students of the BINC, Manchester for their confidence in inviting me to give the Didsbury Lectures. My endeavours to respond to their invitation have proved to be a more rewarding and interesting quest than I had originally anticipated. I am also grateful to Mr. Jeremy Mudditt of the Paternoster Press Ltd. for his willingness to accept the manuscript for publication. I hope that our joint efforts will at least demonstrate to others that there is still a great deal to be learned regarding the inheritance of wisdom from the ancient world.

King's College, London
May 1991

Abbreviations

AARSR	American Academy of Religion Studies in Religion
ATANT	Abhandlungen zur Theologie des Alten und Neuen Testaments
AzT	Arbeiten zur Theologie
BBB	Bonner Biblischer Beiträge
BETL	Bibliotheca Ephemeridum Theologicarum Lovaniensium
BZAW	Beihefte zur Zeitschrift für die alttestamentliche Wissenschaft
CBQ	*Catholic Biblical Quarterly*
ET	English Translation
EvTh	*Evangelische Theologie*
JAAR	*Journal of the American Academy of Religion*
JBL	*Journal of Biblical Literature*
JSOT	*Journal for the Study of the Old Testament*
JSOTSupp	Journal for the Study of the Old Testament Supplement Series
NCB	New Century Bible
NRSV	New Revised Standard Version
OTL	Old Testament Library
OTS	Oudtestamentische Studien
REB	Revised English Bible
RHPR	*Revue d'histoire et de philosophie religieuses*

SBLDS	Society of Biblical Literature Dissertation Series
SBS	Stuttgarter Bibelstudien
SBT	Studies in Biblical Theology
SJT	*Scottish Journal of Theology*
SNTSMS	Society of New Testament Studies Monographs Series
SOTSMS	Society of Old Testament Studies Monographs Series
SUNT	Studien zur Umwelt des Neuen Testaments
ThB	Theologische Bücherei
THAT	*Theologisches Handwörterbuch zum Alten Testament*
TWAT	*Theologische Wörterbuch zum Alten Testament*
UCOP	University of Cambridge Oriental Publications
VTSupp	Supplements to Vetus Testamentum
WMANT	Wissenschaftliche Monographien zum Alten und Neuen Testament

CHAPTER ONE

Introduction

The question of the place that should be assigned to the wisdom writings of the Old Testament in a work of Old Testament theology has not so far been accorded any widely recognized consensus. This is not surprising since the structure and form that such a theology should take has itself been a matter of considerable debate.[1] Whether a purely historical and descriptive approach can suffice, or whether such a theology does not, by its very nature, call for some measure of evaluation, have been issues to which divergent responses have been given. Indeed the whole range of questions concerning the value and effectiveness of the many attempts to reach a truly theological explication of the contents of the Old

---

1. For the study of wisdom the problem has arisen primarily in the wake of W. Eichrodt's attempt to find the normative centre of Old Testament theology in the concept of covenant. For the place of wisdom under such a schematic approach cf. W. Eichrodt, *Theology of the Old Testament*, Vol. II, Eng. Tr. J. A. Baker (London: SCM Press, 1967), pp. 80–92. For the broader issues raised by such an approach cf. H. Graf Reventlow, *Problems of Old Testament Theology in the Twentieth Century*, Eng Tr. John Bowden (London: SCM Press, 1985), pp. 125–133; Gerhard Hasel, *Old Testament Theology. Basic Issues in the Current Debate*, 4th ed. (Grand Rapids: WmB. Eerdmans, 1991), *passim.* Hasel's comments on the theological approaches of G. von Rad, S. Terrien, W. Zimmerli and C. Westermann are especially relevant. Cf. also H. D. Preuss, 'Erwägungen zum theologischen Ort alttestamentlicher Weisheitsliteratur', *EvTh* 30, pp. 393–417; cf. also E. A. Martens 'The Multicolored Landscape of Old Testament Theology', in *The Flowering of Old Testament Theology*, eds. B.C. Ollenburger, E. A. Martens and G. F. Hasel (Winona Lake: Eisenbrauns, 1992), pp. 43–57, esp. pp. 54f.

Testament have aroused responses ranging from enthusiastic pursuit to scholarly indifference. From the outset therefore it is essential to bear in mind that any attempt to consider the lasting theological significance of the wisdom tradition of the Old Testament encounters difficulties. What would be regarded as constituting such a measure of significance will appear very differently in the current diversity of approaches to the task of presenting an Old Testament theology.

A further difficulty faces the researcher in that, in spite of an immense re-awakening of attention to the subject of the Old Testament wisdom writings and the intellectual tradition which gave birth to them, the precise nature and setting of that tradition still remains far from clear.[2] Several fundamental historical uncertainties exist over the degree of importance that ancient Judaism attached to the tradition of wisdom, particularly in its earliest phase of development. Furthermore, both Christians and Jews cannot but be aware that two of the most substantial wisdom writings of the Old Testament, viz. The Teaching of Ben Sira (Ecclesiasticus) and the Wisdom of Solomon are to be found in the Old Testament Apocrypha. This in itself appears to set the wisdom writings in a position of secondary importance since, both through its not being included in most popular printed editions of the Bible and in much biblical preaching, the authority of the Apocrypha is shrouded in a mist of considerable uncertainty. Once we begin to incorporate the structure of the Hebrew canon into an area of primary concern to the methodology of biblical theology, then further problems arise.[3] Furthermore, quite apart from the

---

2. The fullest discussion of the many problems and a full bibliography is given in J. L. Crenshaw, 'The Wisdom Literature', *The Hebrew Bible and Its Modern Interpreters*, eds. D. A. Knight and G. M. Tucker (Philadelphia: Fortress Press/Decatur: Scholars Press, 1985), pp. 369-407. Cf. also J. A. Emerton, 'Wisdom', *Tradition and Interpretation*, ed. G. W. Anderson (Oxford: OUP, 1979), pp. 214-237 and also H. Graf Reventlow, *Problems of Old Testament Theology*, pp. 168–186. For the later Jewish wisdom cf. B. L. Mack and R. E. Murphy 'Wisdom Literature', *Early Judaism and Its Modern Interpreters*, eds. R. A. Kraft and G. W. E. Nickelsburg (Philadelphia: Fortress Press/Atlanta: Scholars Press, 1986), pp. 371–410.

3. The issue is raised in an acute form by the incorporation of the notion of canon as a major structural component of Old Testament theology. Cf. B. S. Childs, *Introduction to the Old Testament as Scripture* (London: SCM Press, 1979), pp. 46–83. It is noteworthy in consequence that wisdom occupies only a relatively minor position in B. S. Childs further elaboration of an Old

significance of these major wisdom writings in the Old Testament Apocrypha, it is arguable that the earlier Hebrew wisdom books may appear, as a consequence of this extensive development of wisdom in these later works, to exhibit the same fringe quality. In spite therefore of a considerable degree of interest in Israelite and Jewish wisdom among biblical scholars this interest cannot be said to have led to any consensus of opinion regarding its distinctive contribution to the growth of the biblical tradition.

Perhaps this needs to be phrased differently, since the truth is that scholars are very divided over the question of the centrality and significance of the wisdom tradition for Jewish and Christian religious development. Earlier critical opinion has usually placed it on the margins of both traditions, and only in recent research has this been countered by a contrasting claim that its role was more fundamental to the formation of ethical and theological ideas.[4] In particular it has been argued that wisdom marks the most truly intellectual and theological dimension of the impact of ancient Israelite religion upon the subsequent rise of Judaism and Christianity. Certainly it can now be agreed that the extent of wisdom's impact upon the growth of the earliest Christian tradition had previously been widely underestimated and insufficiently recognized. Whether this must be taken to imply that Jesus himself can more properly be described as a teacher of wisdom than an apocalyptic revolutionary, is not the primary issue.[5] More important for the structure of a biblical theology is the growing realization that a number of inherited lines of theological thought, drawn from the Jewish wisdom tradition, served to shape Christian theological and ethical thinking.

Testament theology along canonical lines in *Old Testament Theology, in a Canonical Context* (London: SCM Press, 1985), pp. 210–212; cf. also p. 232. A critique of such attempts at a canonical approach to the problems of biblical theology is set out in M. Oeming, *Gesamt biblische Theologien der Gegenwart* (Stuttgart: W. Kohlhammer, 1985), pp. 186ff.

4. Cf. especially, H. H. Schmid, 'Creation, Righteousness and Salvation as the Broad Horizon of Biblical Theology', *Creation in The Old Testament*, ed. B. W. Anderson (London: SPCK, 1984), pp. 102–117. Cf. also J. J. Collins, 'The Biblical Precedent for Natural Theology, *JAAR* 45, 1977, pp. 35–62.

5. Cf. Burton L. Mack, *A Myth of Innocence. Mark and Christian Origins* (Philadelphia: Fortress Press, 1988); cf. also his essay 'The Kingdom Sayings in Mark', *FORUM. Foundations and Facets* Vol. 3, 1987, pp. 3–47.

The Wisdom Tradition and Its Ancient Near Eastern Background

We may commence our examination of the theological significance of Old Testament wisdom by noting the literature with which we are primarily concerned. This consists of the Book of Proverbs, which remains the oldest and most central collection of ancient Israelite wisdom teaching, and the Books of Job and Qoheleth (Ecclesiastes). In the Apocrypha, as already mentioned, the writing of Ben Sira and the book known as The Wisdom of Solomon will occupy rather less of our attention. There are reasons for this, of which the chief is that the former shows itself to have been profoundly influenced by a concern to accommodate and conflate the teaching of wisdom with a received and established tradition of sacred scripture built around the concept of *torah* (popularly translated 'law', but more broadly to be understood as 'divine instruction').

The second writing, that of the Wisdom of Solomon, is of a very different kind and reveals a considerable measure of assimilation to Hellenism with its philosophical interests and methods. Both can properly be described as wisdom writings, but each of them shows how the original style, assumptions and forms of wisdom which were rooted in the ancient Near East came to be modified by new factors which profoundly influenced later Judaism.[6] In consequence the earliest features of Israelite wisdom have become so modified by later concerns that, although they are still present to some degree, the characteristic theological aims of wisdom are less prominently to be seen. Wisdom has become mixed with other interests so that its formative impulses have been overlaid and changed.

In addition to these writings we should note that certain psalms, especially Pss. 1, 37, 73, 104 and 119, display a measure of influence from wisdom.[7] Similarly such influence

---

6. Cf. M. Hengel, *Judaism and Hellenism*, 2 vols. Eng. Tr. John Bowden (London: SCM Press, 1974), especially Vol. I, pp. 107–175. See also Burton L. Mack, *Logos und Sophia: Untersuchungen zur Weisheitstheologie in hellenistischen Judentum*, SUNT 10 (Göttingen: Vandenhoeck & Ruprecht, 1973).

7. Cf. S. Mowinckel, 'Psalms and Wisdom', *Wisdom in Israel and the Ancient Near East*, eds. H. H. Rowley & D. Winton Thomas, VTSupp III

has frequently been discerned by modern scholars in various of the prophetic writings, notably Amos and Isaiah.[8] That both legal formulations and historical narratives also received some degree of influence from traditions of wisdom is highly probable and widely accepted among scholars.

This Israelite wisdom tradition displays characteristics which establish its affinity with a much wider search for wisdom and understanding in the ancient Near East. Most prominently this tradition is evidenced in Egypt, although a substantial body of didactic literature exists from ancient Sumeria and Babylon, and the Old Testament itself points to a tradition of wisdom among the Edomites (Obadiah 8).

We can accept that, with appropriate local variations, the search for wisdom and understanding was a very widespread feature of the nations and cities that emerged in the ancient Near East from as far back as the fourth millenium BCE. To what extent this feature of ancient civilisation passed directly from one community to another, and how far it displayed the marks of parallel quests emerging among different groups is not wholly clear. Certainly there are abundant indications that the search for such wisdom and its application to daily life represented a significant feature that accompanied the spread of urban civilisation from the time of the rise of Sumerian power.

The centre of attention for the study of Old Testament wisdom is primarily to be found in the Book of Proverbs. This represents a collection of wisdom teaching which reaches back to its ancient origins in Israel and which has been made in order to preserve, in distilled fashion, its major insights. Like the Psalter to which it is a companion, it is in reality a collection of collections, made and edited over a considerable period of time.[9] Among these the two largest are comprised of Prov. 1:1–

(Leiden: E. J. Brill, 1955), pp. 205–224. J. K. Kuntz, 'The Canonical Wisdom Psalms of Ancient Israel: Their Rhetorical, Thematic and Formal Dimensions', *Rhetorical Criticism. Essays in Honor of James Muilenburg*, ed. J. J. Jackson and M. Kessler, Pittsburgh Theological Monographs 1, (Pittsburgh: The Pickwick Press, 1974), pp. 186–222.

8. Cf. Donn F. Morgan, *Wisdom in The Old Testament Traditions* (Atlanta: John Knox, 1981).

9. H. Gese, 'Wisdom Literature in the Persian Period', *The Cambridge History of Judaism*, Vol. 1, eds. W. D. Davies and L. Finkelstein

9:18 and 10:1–22:16. We are entitled to assume that the book has been compiled both to preserve the best of what wisdom had to teach about life and human duty and also to fulfil a specific practical function. Further shorter collections are to be found in Prov. 22:17–24:22; 25:1–29:27; 30:1–33 and 31:1–31.

Both in their form as independent collections, and in their final form as a book, proverbs appear to have been intended to be used as a teaching resource. Probably the original shorter independent collections were directed at a narrower readership than is the case for the completed book. A strong case can also be made for concluding that the material in Prov. 1–9 was intended to provide a broadly based introduction to the older collections which follow. Some of this material appears actually to have been composed to fulfil such an introductory purpose, while other parts may have enjoyed an earlier independent existence. Accordingly the several disquisitions upon the nature, and life-encompassing, role of wisdom which appear were aimed at bolstering its claim to provide a major compendium of truth and reflection from which everyone could derive benefit. These goals have undoubtedly influenced the selection of material and the emphases of its contents. There is a general impression given that the earlier wisdom may have been targeted at a narrower audience group than is true of the book of Proverbs in its final form.

Following a widely adopted conclusion among scholars, we may accept that wisdom first emerged in Israel in the pre-exilic-period. Many, indeed, have been inclined to adhere to the Israelite historical tradition that the age of Solomon, if not the actual person of the king, marked the beginning of the Israelite wisdom tradition.[10] This may be the case to the extent that the emergence of a powerful and ambitious monarch with a strong central administration provided the conditions under which the nurture of wisdom could flourish. It is very improbable, however, that the person of Solomon as an individual was more

---

(Cambridge: CUP, 1984), pp. 189–218, identifies 9 major collections in the Book of Proverbs, viz. 1) 1:1–9:18; 2) 10:1–22:16; 3) 22:17–24:32; 4) 24:23–34; 5) 25:1–29:27; 6) 30:1–14; 7) 30:15–33; 8) 31:1–9; 9) 31:10–31.

10. For a discussion of the various attempts to establish a Solomonic origin for wisdom in Israel see my article 'Solomon and the Origins of Wisdom in Israel', *Perspectives in Religious Studies* 15, 1988, pp. 23–36.

than a figurehead to which the ascription of outstanding wisdom could be attached.[11]

So far as our present study is concerned we may follow the widely adopted conclusion that the main period of the Israelite growth and spread of wisdom was in the post-exilic era, when Judah was living under Persian rule.[12] This era, so far as the extant literary tradition of the Book of Proverbs is concerned, was one in which serious efforts were undertaken to record and develop a distinctively Jewish tradition of wisdom. Undoubtedly elements of a far older sapiental tradition were retained, but so also were a number of quite distinctively Jewish characteristics imposed onto wisdom.[13] No longer was it a rather broad and indeterminate tradition of guidance and insight, but it acquired all the features of a distinctively Jewish garment. It became part of the tradition concerning the revealed will of the Lord (YHWH), the God of Judaism, and it took on features which were strikingly distinctive, when compared with the inherited themes and concepts of its older oriental antecedents. The search for wisdom became a quest for an authentically Jewish affirmation of theological and ethical truth. Inevitably this demanded accommodation to the demands set forth in the *torah*—the Jewish formulation of law—but its ideas and methods displayed considerable differences from those which governed the composition of the written *torah*. To an extent the eventual form of the *torah* squeezed out any continuing demand for a separate tradition of wisdom and, in any case, other historical eventualities intervened to push wisdom to the margins of Jewish life. Nevertheless, the very processes which shaped the written *torah* owed no little debt to the style of reasoning engendered by the wisdom tradition.

---

11. Solomon's association with the origins of Israelite wisdom are best understood as indicative of the strong link between wisdom and the political theory of the state, rather than with the closeness of Israelite cultural indebtedness to Egypt (as E. W. Heaton, *Solomon's New Men*, London: Batsford, 1974) or with any distinctively charismatic tradition of Solomon's learning (as A. Alt, 'Die Weisheit Salomos', *Kleine Schriften* II, Munich, 1953, pp. 90–99).
12. Cf. especially the valuable survey by H. Gese remarked in note 9 above.
13. The classic study remains that by J. Fichtner, *Die altorientalische Weisheit in ihrer israelitisch-jüdischen Ausprägung. Eine Studie zur National-isierung der Weisheit in Israel*, BZAW 62 (Giessen: Töpelmann, 1933).

The Distinctiveness of Wisdom in Israelite Life

So far as the presentation of an Old Testament theology is concerned, we may draw attention to the prime reason why wisdom has appeared to be a fringe, and almost an alien, element within it.[14] In seeking to establish a co-ordinating structure for such a theology, W. Eichrodt focussed attention upon the concept of a covenant between God and his people Israel. God was known as One who had bound himself in covenant to Israel as her Lord. He was Yahweh, the God of Israel. Israel in turn was to be known, and to shape its destiny, as the people of this God. So the concept of covenant carried with it belief in the divine election of Israel, highlighting the uniqueness of the constitution of Israel given in the *torah*. The making of this covenant provided the focal centre of the historical narratives recounting Israel's national origins.

Startlingly, references to such a covenant and election are absent in the earliest wisdom teaching. Instead this wisdom addresses itself to individual human beings as members of the human race, irrespective of their nationality, and it appeals for its authority to the experienced order of the world as it has been created. Accordingly ideas of an ordered creation, and of the universal applicability of the teachings of wisdom, contrast with the emphasis upon God's unique actions towards Israel in Old Testament prophecy and historical writings. In the very formative application of the concept of *torah* by the Deuteronomists to describe God's revelation, this is specifically presented as truth uniquely vouchsafed to Israel (cf. Deut. 4:32–40). Contrastingly wisdom is proudly offered to the inquiring spirit of every nation.

Moreover a further feature that has appeared prejudicial to locating wisdom in a central position in an Old Testament theology has been the demonstrable fact that its origins can be clearly traced outside of Israel. Its beginnings in the ancient

---

14. Many of the points noted are set out in the study by W. Zimmerli 'The Place and Limit of Wisdom in the Framework of Old Testament Theology', *SJT* 17, 1964, pp. 146–158 (More fully in the original German essay reprinted in *Gottes Offenbarung. Gesammelte Aufsätze*, ThB 19, (Munich: Kaiser Verlag, 1963), pp. 300–315. Cf. also the same author's treatment in *Old Testament Theology in Outline*, Eng. Tr. D. E. Green (Atlanta: John Knox Press, 1978), pp. 155–166.

Near East far antedate the time of Moses. More strikingly a very close link is discernible between certain Israelite wisdom sayings and parallels from the surrounding world.[15]

We can add the yet further point that wisdom asserted that its truths were based on observation and experience, which could be tested by honest and critical scrutiny. This is so unlike the stress on revealed divine authority which marks priestly and prophetic tradition. For prophecy to be regarded as a 'true' disclosure of the divine will it required to have been given by a figure endowed with charismatic authority from God. In contrast to this wisdom appealed for its authority to the evidence of experience and the results of verifiable observation. Only at a late stage did there emerge ideas concerning a 'hidden' wisdom which was unavailable to all but a few individuals blessed with special insight and knowledge.

In its understanding of how truth is revealed and perceived, wisdom made very distinctive assumptions of its own. Accordingly the preserved teachings of wisdom, in the style of their presentation and their claims to be listened to, convey a very different manner of appeal, from those of either prophecy or priesthood. It is not surprising therefore that wisdom has often appeared to be a-religious, and at times even bordering on the secular, in its approach to life. The overall impression concerning wisdom has therefore been of a profoundly interesting, and at times challenging, feature of ancient Israelite culture, but one which was in most respects marginal to the growth and development of Israel's religion.[16]

A further feature is very important for the understanding of

---

15. The most notable instance of this has been the close correspondence between much of Prov. 22:17–24:22 and the Egyptian Teaching of Amen-em-ope. However, irrespective of this specific instance, the rich compass of ancient oriental wisdom and its links with the Old Testament can be readily seen by careful investigation. Cf. Glendon E. Bryce, *A Legacy of Wisdom. The Egyptian Contribution to the Wisdom of Israel* (Lewisburg: Bucknell University Press, 1979); E. Würthwein, 'Die Weisheit Ägyptens und das Alte Testament', *Wort und Existenz* (Göttingen: Vandenhoeck & Ruprecht, 1970), pp. 197–216. (ET 'Egyptian Wisdom and the Old Testament' in *Studies in Ancient Israelite Wisdom*, ed. J. L. Crenshaw (New York: Ktav, 1976), pp. 113–133.

16. This is readily apparent by observing the quite marginal place ascribed to wisdom in the Old Testament theological writings of W. Zimmerli, B. S. Childs and others.

the incorporation of a tradition of wisdom teaching into Israelite life. In Egypt *maat*, a close counterpart to wisdom, was linked to the political order and structure of the state. There had arisen the conviction that this political structure was inseparably interconnected with a divine order imposed upon the world at creation. This in turn determined the economic and moral order of society so that *maat* was inseparably linked to the monarchic structure of economic and political life. Inevitably this came to be expressed in traditions which propagated the belief in a distinctive royal wisdom. Much has accordingly been written on the role played by the royal court, both in Egypt and in Israel, in the collection, composition and dissemination of wisdom instruction.[17]

That such a tradition of royal wisdom existed in pre-exilic Israel is fully accepted as fundamental to these studies. At the same time, it cannot be overlooked that there existed an older, more popular and more diverse, tradition of wisdom which had its roots among the general populace and in the morality, conventions and intellectual pursuits of rural family life. This tradition of a more widespread kind of folk wisdom, embodying both practical injunctions for daily conduct and also artistic use of language and poetry, displays many of the most basic and formative features of wisdom teaching.

Since post-exilic Israel no longer enjoyed the governmental privileges of a royal house of its own, it is evident that the Jewish wisdom teaching, of this period, which represents the era of wisdom's fullest literary development so far as the Old Testament is concerned, spread its claims far beyond the immediate circle of the royal court. Even when this is interpreted to comprehend not only the senior head of government but a larger circle of administrative officials and governors, it is clear that wisdom offered its insights to communities which ranged far outside a privileged court minority.

We may use as a provisional assumption therefore the outline picture that Israelite wisdom passed through three distinct

---

17. Cf. N. W. Porteous, 'Royal Wisdom', *Living The Mystery. Collected Essays* (Oxford: B. H. Blackwell, 1967), pp. 77–91.

phases.[18] The first of these is, of necessity, the least definable and clearcut in its character. It concerned the earliest Israelite traditions of folk wisdom. This emerged within families and clans and provided both practical advice and intellectual stimulus. It incorporated several aspects of family life, being pragmatic and strongly respectful of the authority of the family headed by the father. It also encouraged artistic elaboration in the form of riddles, allegories, fables and other forms of poetic speech. The fact that the proverb (Heb. *mashal*—'likeness') remained one of the most popular and basic of all forms of wisdom utterance suggests that skilful use of metaphor and simile were favoured features of wisdom teaching.[19] This points to the conclusion that the combination of artistic originality with moral practicality belonged to wisdom instruction from its earliest identifiable beginnings in Israel.

That, during the period of the monarchy in Israel, wisdom came to be especially nurtured in the royal court and to be closely associated with court life and etiquette explains how wisdom passed into a second phase. This does not require that wisdom became exclusively a prerogative of the royal court and its administrators, but that it underwent very formative changes in this context. Wisdom took on much of the character of 'royal wisdom' in which the king was accorded very high respect as an exponent of wisdom and when the contents of this sapiental instruction came to incorporate a strong national and political dimension.

Clearly this period of wisdom's close association with the royal court affected it in several ways. It introduced into it forthright pro-monarchic sentiments and gave to it a political dimension which the earlier folk wisdom had lacked. Yet it was not in matters of content alone that we may confidently assume that wisdom's connections with monarchy manifested themselves. It is highly probable that during this period wisdom achieved far greater artistic sophistication. Moreover adoption

---

18. For a recognition of this threefold pattern of wisdom development in Israel, cf. Peter Doll, *Menschenschöpfung und Weltschöpfung in der alttestamentlichen Weisheit*, SBS 117 (Stuttgart: Katholisches Bibelwerk, 1985), pp. 7ff. It is, however, fundamental to much recent perception concerning the nature of Israelite wisdom.
19. For the meaning of Heb. *mashal* cf. K.-M. Beyse, *TWAT*, Bd. V, 69–73.

by administrators and association with administrative procedures must certainly have encouraged wisdom to take on a literary form. From being an oral teaching it was given new shape in literary collections, a development which Egyptian evidence amply shows to have already occurred there. This literary reshaping itself served to encourage greater artistic elaboration and brought about substantial changes of form.

The appearance in Prov. 22:17–24:22 of material drawn from the Egyptian Teaching of Amenemope illustrates this literary phase of development. It also strongly suggests that this may very well have been the period of greatest Israelite openness to the other sapiental traditions of the ancient Near East.[20] We can confidently draw the conclusion therefore that much of what is now preserved in Prov. 10–31 represents collections of sayings and teachings which originated during the period of the monarchy among circles which stood close to the royal court.

The third phase of Israelite wisdom development occurred after the exile. This was undoubtedly the most consistently literary stage of wisdom's growth, producing such a priceless literary jewel as the Book of Job. It also witnessed the composition of the longer didactic poems of Prov. 1–9 and led to the collection and literary shaping of the Book of Proverbs as a whole.[21] By the latter half of the third century BCE the author of the biblical book of Ecclesiastes (Qoheleth) was active and reflecting deeply and provocatively upon Judaism's inherited tradition of wisdom. By this time the first strong impulses of Hellenistic teaching were affecting Jewish life, posing a strong counter-attraction to the increasing conservatism and rigidity of a more traditionally pious community of Jews.

It is this third, post-exilic, phase of the development of wisdom in Israel which will occupy most of our attention. The

20. Cf. H. H. Schmid, *Wesen und Geschichte der Weisheit. Eine Untersuchung zur altorientalischen und israelitischen Weisheitsliteratur*, BZAW 101, (Berlin: De Gruyter, 1966).
21. The attempt of C. Kayatz, *Studien zu Proverbien 1–9*, WMANT XXII, (Neukirchen-Vluyn: Neukirchener Verlag, 1966) to press for a pre-exilic date on the basis of the closeness to certain Egyptian parallels does not take adequate account of the many distinctively Israelite features in the contents of Prov. 1–9.

reasons for this lie in the fact that it is this period that has brought about the embodiment of wisdom in a fixed literary form. The primary theological characteristics of Old Testament wisdom are essentially therefore a product of developments that took place at this time. Although we are entitled to conclude that these developments were genuinely respectful of the need to retain sayings and teachings from the pre-exilic era, we must recognize that this work of preservation was also one of reshaping and addition. Wisdom was being given a more coherent and consistent form which has finally determined its canonical shape.

It is also our argument that it was at this time that wisdom came to make its most meaningful and lasting contribution to Israel's intellectual life. The reason for this is not difficult to find, for it was in this period that Israel was forced to make the transition from being a nation-state to becoming a scattered diaspora among many nations. Whereas Israelite religion had originally reflected Israel's national identity, the newly emerging religion of Judaism was of necessity forced to be more international in character. The dimension of national identity came almost wholly to be subsumed as part of a prophetic eschatology.[22] A return to Israel's condition as a nation-state was projected into the future as a feature of the hope for the bringing to full fruition of the expectations implicit in the notion of a divinely chosen and blessed people.

For the present Israel had to learn to live as a community which was physically divided and scattered among many nations. Moreover, even in Judah it failed to regain full sovereignty over its own affairs. On this account the very fact that wisdom offered the most truly universalist and international body of teaching about life, morality and the nature of reality, made it the natural resource for coping with the new situation. For a time wisdom held a unique key to understanding the new world in which Jews found themselves among the

---

22. For this development cf. H. G. M. Williamson, 'The Concept of Israel in Transition', *The World of Ancient Israel*, ed. R. E. Clements (Cambridge: CUP, 1989), pp. 141–162. For the political background cf. Eric M. Meyers, 'The Persian Period and the Judean Restoration: From Zerubbabel to Nehemiah', *Ancient Israelite Religion. FS Frank M. Cross*, Jr., Eds. P. D. Miller, Jr., P. Hanson and S. Dean McBride (Philadelphia: Fortress Press, 1987), pp. 509–521.

nations. This was the period when the concept of *torah* was developed further to provide a basis of teaching which could be observed both in Judah and amongst Jews of the dispersion. In this process a strong wisdom influence can be discerned.[23]

Whether we think of the pressures of this situation of diaspora as primarily threatening, and therefore calling for an apologetic of faith, or opportunistic and positive, Jews found themselves in need of fresh intellectual resources. These had to base their moral and social norms in the experienced world in all its fullness, rather than in Israel's national origins at Mount Sinai. Yet the authoritative and established traditions which the Jews of the diaspora took with them, and which we find in the Deuteronomic and Deuteronomistic literature, were framed within this national ideology.

The very notion of covenant, with all its varied connotations, was weakened because it affirmed that Yahweh had made a covenant with Israel as a nation (so especially Exod. 19:5–6). Just as directly the royal covenant with the house of David presupposed the national structure of Israel as a community. Over against such intellectual orientation Jewish existence among the nations called for ideas and teachings which were authentic to Israel, and yet truly universal in their validity. For Jews these conditions could most readily be met by the tradition of wisdom. Such wisdom had ancient roots in Israelite life, and yet did not appeal for the authority and truth of its teachings to a unique revelation vouchsafed to Israel as a nation at the decisive moment of its origin.

Wisdom in a Liminal Society

In studies relating the importance of experiences of Christian pilgrimage to those of *rites de passage* in primitive societies, the anthropologist Victor Turner has pointed to the great religious significance of experiences involving a condition of liminality.[24] In this there is a temporary suspension of normal

---

23. Cf. E. Würthwein, 'Der Sinn des Gesetzes im Alten Testament', *Wort und Existenz*, pp. 39–54, (= *ZThK* 55, 1958, pp. 255–270) esp. pp. 52ff.
24. Cf. Leo G. Perdue, 'Liminality as a Social Setting for Wisdom Instructions', *ZAW* 93 (1981), pp. 114–126. V. Turner, *The Ritual Process. Structure and Anti-Structure*, (Chicago: Aldine Pub. Co., 1969), pp. 94ff.; cf. also V. & E. Turner, *Image and Pilgrim in Christian Culture. Anthropological*

relationships and their accompanying perceptions, closely related to entry into a new social environment. The experience is one of transition, initially in primitive societies at puberty, from a juvenile to an adult world. In this those who pass through such rites undergo a very strong sense of bonding to those with whom they share the experience. There is also a measure of distancing from an earlier phase of life and a sense of appropriating new goals and responsibilities which serve to shape future activities. The whole period is one in which existence becomes liminal—reaching up to the margins of established patterns and norms, and providing the opportunity for profound changes of attitude and understanding.

Turner's extension of these insights regarding *rites de passage* to cover pilgrimage experiences made at any time draws attention to the manner in which a condition of liminality affects human perceptions and attitudes at many stages of life. Furthermore such a condition provides the opportunity for a significant reminting of values and aims which have a most profound consequence for human existence. Even conditions entered into unwillingly under situations of social duress may nonetheless prove to be formative in a very positive way for individuals and larger communities.

The point is capable of being pressed further, and is of direct relevance to the study of Old Testament wisdom. It is such periods of experiencing the conditions of liminality which are of immense importance for the introduction and appropriation of significant changes of thought and attitude. The experience of liminality can be life transforming. This is a point that will be fully familiar to all who have worked in the organizing of pilgrimages, youth camps, and similar activities where fundamentally new, if temporary, environments are provided for people out of a concern to promote a deepened religious perceptiveness.

Our suggestion is that it is this condition of liminality which can best describe the situation of those Jews who passed, after

Perspectives (New York: Columbia UP, 1978), pp. 1–39; 'Passages, Margins and Poverty. Religious Symbols of Communitas', *Dramas, Fields and Metaphors* (Ithaca: Cornell Univ. Press, 1974), pp. 231–271. I am indebted to Perdue's suggestions, but have sought to extend the relevance of the concept of liminality to wisdom studies far beyond that which he has noted.

587 BCE, from an established world, made meaningful by a
sense of national identity, into the new world of the Jewish
dispersion.[25] The primary reason for applying this concept lies
in its appropriateness to defining the historical reality of what
took place for Judaism after 587 BCE. The destruction of the
Jerusalem temple and the loss of a national ruling monarch
gave birth to a new, and profoundly influential, period of
Jewish development. This began with many former Judean
citizens being forced into a state of 'exile' (Heb. *golah*) and
found its primary focus among those Jews who had been taken
to Babylon by Nebuchadnezzar in 598 BCE. They formed a
hostage community in Babylon, later to be joined by others
after 587 BCE. The usual fate of such unfortunates would have
been a slow atrophying of community identity, a high mortality
rate, and gradual assimilation for the hardier and more resilient
into the new society to which they had been taken. Such a
threatened fate of 'death among the nations' is well described in
numerous prophetic sayings from the books of the prophets
Jeremiah and Ezekiel (cf. Jer. 8:3; 16:13; 17:4; Ezek. 6:8–10,
12; 12:6). Exile was conventionally recognized as a slow form
of death. Its victims were in constant danger of becoming non-
persons, unless they were fortunate enough to be able to
assume a fresh identity in the alien environment to which they
had been taken.

Strikingly, however, this did not happen, at least for a
significant proportion of the Jews of the dispersion. Their early
expectations of a return to the homeland kept alive a measure of
personal hope; but, more surprisingly, their life in exile
appears gradually to have become tolerable and to have taken
on a relatively stable form. More surprisingly still, this new
mode of existence came to be defended and accepted as part of a
divine plan to rebuild a new Israel in the future. Religious and
personal identity were not lost, but were instead redefined and
expressed in new ways. In consequence a significantly new

---

25. The early origins and development of diaspora Judaism out of a
condition of exile remain shrouded in much obscurity. For valuable outline
sketches of the transition from exile to a more established pattern of
dispersion cf. E. J. Bickerman, The Diaspora B. The Babylonian Captivity',
The Cambridge History of Judaism, Vol. 1, pp. 342–357; R. J. Coggins, 'The
Origins of the Jewish Diaspora', *The World of Ancient Israel*, pp. 163–181.

dimension of Israelite religion was born as the faith and practice of communities in exile.[26]

It is this condition of exile that we can usefully describe as one of liminality. Jews found themselves brought to the frontiers of human existence, respecting the past and hoping for a better future, but meanwhile being compelled to re-think and redefine what it meant to be the people of God. Prominent among the issues which such exiled Jews had to face were those concerning the most basic ideas of the nature of physical and territorial reality. Originally Israel's spatial concepts had been presented symbolically as part of a cultic world-view which centered upon the Jerusalem temple. The inhabited environment was interpreted as one of sacred space, rendered knowable and acceptable by the rituals which ensured its holiness and purity. This quality of holiness was affirmed through the mythological symbolism of cult artefacts and traditions, and was upheld and renewed seasonally through various rituals. For early Israel direct participation in the cult had been a fundamental part of establishing an ordered and friendly world, as is shown by the requirement that all males should present themselves before God at least three times during the year (Exod. 23:17; 34:23).

We cannot interpret the significance of early Israelite worship therefore simply in the individualistic categories of private piety. The cult was a vital ingredient for the establishing of the intellectual horizons of the daily life of the entire nation. Existence could not be divorced from cultus, and this in turn could not be separated from the imagery and symbolism of a mythological world-view which was affirmed through psalmody and ritual. In this fashion Israel's national existence was believed to be upheld through the rites of the cultus. The 'Songs of Zion' were the songs through which Israel affirmed its national identity, and through which it sought to preserve its welfare.

For those carried away into exile all this had gone, so that loss of access to the Jerusalem temple worship was not simply the deprivation of an inner world of spiritual renewal and

---

26. The immense contribution of the experience of dispersion to the formation of Judaism as we know it was fully recognised by A. Causse in his studies 'Les origines de la diaspora juive', *RHPR* 7, 1927, pp. 97–128; *Les*

comfort. It was the taking away of the most central elements of mental furniture. It plunged Jews, torn from their homeland in Judah, into a new world of liminality. The response to the new situation demanded a completely fresh intellectual geography. Such a condition must initially have led to a period of disorientation and loss of identity until a new world-view, appropriate to existence in an alien country and culture, could be acquired.

Certainly scholarship has long recognized the profound changes that came into Israelite worship as a result of the experience of exile and the birth of the Jewish dispersion.[27] Such institutions as sabbath observance and circumcision took on deeper significance and a more inward and individualistic type of piety emerged in which psalmody rather than sacrifice became the central feature. The tracing of such changes has long been of concern to historical scholarship. However two factors have tended to minimise its impact.

The first of these has been the tendency to study the post-587 era in a manner which places the greatest emphasis upon the restoration of Jewish worship and political life in Jerusalem after the collapse of Babylonian rule. Undoubtedly this development was of major significance yet it was only a partial achievement and was unable to restore the situation to what it had been prior to 587 BCE for a variety of reasons. Although the temple of Jerusalem was rebuilt, Israel had not recovered its separate identity as a nation. To some degree therefore the very notion of a post-exilic period is fraught with incongruities. For an ever increasing number of Jews the state of exile did not come to an end. It simply passed, by a series of gradual social and political changes, into a condition of relatively permanent dispersion. Consequently even the restoration of worship and administrative leadership in the Jerusalem temple remained only a distant and notional reality for a large numbers of Jews whose political world remained physically separate from this.

Disperses d'Israël: les origines de la Diaspora et son rôle dans la formation de Judaisme, (Paris: Alcan, 1929); *Du groupe ethnique à la communauté religieuse; le probleme sociologique de la religion d'Israel* (Paris: Alcan, 1937).
27. Cf. P. R. Ackroyd, *Exile and Restoration. A Study of Hebrew Thought of the Sixth Century BC*, (London: SCM Press, 1968), pp. 232ff.

We can see therefore that, although with the arrival of Persian rule after 538 BCE the time of most immediate crisis had passed, the period of exile had not come to an end. Rather the temporary conditions which had pertained under Babylonian rule provided the norm for a more permanent situation under the Persians. As these changes took place, the insights which had been attained and approved in the liminal conditions of exile established the groundwork for further new religious developments. What had begun as a system of temporary and make-do concessions to a situation that had initally been regarded as purely transitory became part of a relatively permanent state of religious affairs. The period of the Babylonian exile was, to all intents and purposes, the period of withdrawal and transition which gave rise to a greatly changed intellectual world of Judaism.

In this the increasing importance to Jewish life of a written *torah* to govern present activity, and the relegation to a prophetic eschatology of the traditions of national election and national destiny, were the most significant changes that occurred.

The Literary Development of Wisdom

The primary means by which Jews sought to come to terms with the experience of national dissolution and catastrophe occasioned by what took place in 587 BCE was through the word of prophecy.[28] Most notably here we can place the work of the two great exilic prophets, Jeremiah and Ezekiel. Yet the Book of Isaiah also shows in its complex structure that it too has been shaped by an awareness of the impact of the events of 598 and 587 BCE. Furthermore, in its overall canonical shape, the Book of the Twelve Prophets pivots upon the events that transpired for Israel and Judah at the hands of the Babylonians.

In general it can be claimed that this word of prophecy, originally in spoken form, but now recorded and edited to become a literature, provided a message of theodicy and legitimation. It represented a formula of theodicy insofar as it sought to present reasons why God's sovereign will had

---

28. Cf. P. R. Ackroyd, *ibid.*, pp. 50ff., 103ff.

demanded the downfall of Israel and the destruction of the temple of Jerusalem. At the same time it also forms a literature of legitimation in that it adumbrates new patterns and priorities which show how Israel may hope to recover its lost land and national identity. It further supports this by outlining a way of loyalty and devotion to God which will enable Israel to maintain its special divine relationship in the painful interim period before full national restoration is achieved.

Yet this written word of prophecy remained too limited in its scope and too varied in its focus on specific issues and concerns to offer a rounded restructuring of Israel's intellectual heritage. It served to authorise a pattern of worship separate from that of the earlier temple cultus and established the framework of hope and eschatology which justified the present conditions of exile as a period of liminality. It did not, however, set out detailed guidance for the wider range of daily issues concerned with health, work, family morality and the relevance of religion to daily life. For this a more distinctive body of tradition, not moulded and shaped by the concepts and symbolism of the cultus, was required. It is this that wisdom provided.

This hitherto rather narrow and privileged stream of Israelite intellectual life offered the intellectual resources necessary to deal with a situation of liminality. Once prophecy had provided the *raison d'être* for the coming into being of the state of dispersion, and the physical distancing of a majority of Jews from the formal temple cultus, wisdom laid out the basis for a more far reaching reminting of the Israelite world-view. No longer was this to be drawn from the mythology and traditions associated with the Jerusalem temple worship, but from the concept of a world order established at creation by God through the exercise of wisdom.

We have already noted that Israelite wisdom came to exercise its most distinctive influence during the Persian period. This is undoubtedly the most probable conclusion to be drawn from the literary structure of the Book of Proverbs. It represents the oldest and most wide-ranging of the writings of wisdom contained in the Old Testament. Consequently it is the one which will most directly occupy our attention in examining the presuppositions of Israelite wisdom and its contribution to Old Testament theology.

We have already noted that the book of Proverbs is a collection of collections which still establish identifiable units within the whole. The major core of the work, and the collection which contains the oldest material, is to be found in Prov. 10:1–22:21. These admonitions and sayings date from the period before the exile, although it appears highly probable that some later revisions have been made to them. The purpose of such revisions would have been to accommodate the older wisdom into the more unified and precisely defined aims of the post-exilic period.

The contents of Prov. 1–9, however, are certainly from the post-exilic age, some from as late as the Hellenistic era. Certain of the longer expositions of the value and comprehensiveness of wisdom which these chapters contain appear to have been composed to provide an introduction to 10:1ff. Other parts appear once to have existed as independent units. Most notably the lengthy, and artistically elaborate, disquisition on the primary role of wisdom in creation contained in Prov. 8:1–36. This possesses a markedly apologetic character, not so much celebrating wisdom's role in unlocking the mysteries of creation as affirming the belief that creation itself endorsed the truth of wisdom's claims. It displays a strongly assertive character, rather unlike the more typical 'look and see for yourself' appeals of the older shorter wisdom admonitions.

Other old collections of wisdom sayings, identified by their separate superscriptions, are to be found in Prov. 22:22–31:31. These may well have originated before 587 BCE, although their date, and places, of origin are unclear. We may claim, in any case, that it belongs to the very nature of many forms of wisdom saying that they should address the human situation in its broad commonality, and consequently lack specific historical connections. Furthermore the constant possibility of adaptation and minor revision means that any attempt to insist on a specific date of origin for wisdom sayings is fraught with difficulty. All we can hope to achieve is the tracing of some broad lines of development.

The Book of Job, undoubtedly the richest literary jewel in the crown of the biblical wisdom literature, probably origin-

ated in the Persian era. Its concern with the specific theme of
human suffering means that it will occupy our attention rather
less than the other wisdom writings, even though it presupposes the kind of extensive development of wisdom in the
Persian age that forms a central part of our thesis. More
directly relevant to its concern with central questions of human
existence is its focusing upon the experience of illness as a part
of the mystery of human suffering. In doing so it presupposes
that such illness derives from God, and yet is largely to be
separated from the province of the cult and from questions of
uncleanness and levitical purity. It treats disease as a matter of
human distress, and no longer as a primary concern of cultic
purity and holiness.

The Book of Qoheleth belongs to the late third century BCE,
and reveals the first traces of the influence of Greek popular
philosophy and didactic fashions upon Jewish life. More than
most of the earlier wisdom it marks substantially the work of a
single author and bears a very distinctive, and at times
idiosyncratic, stamp. Its author draws upon the older wisdom
teaching, displaying a perceptively critical attitude to many of
its over-confident assertions. At the same time, the extent of
the influence upon him of the Greek Stoic philosophers appears
more in manner and style, than in essential content.

In two directions Qoheleth marks a significant milestone in
the progress of wisdom. In the first place there are clear signs
that, although the author was accustomed to delivering his
teaching orally, he has developed characteristically literary
structures and woven short epigrammatic sayings into more
extended compositions. Individual sayings have been combined into larger structures which serve to modify, and even
challenge, the validity of the shorter individual sayings. Some
sections display the form of asserting a thesis, seemingly
outrageous, which is then skilfully justified (cf. the saying
about the day of death being preferable to the day of birth;
Qoh. 7:1–8). Secondly it appears that Qoheleth was concerned
to set out a sufficiently comprehensive attitude to life that it
could properly be regarded as a form of personal philosophy.
The older wisdom quest for a comprehensive understanding of
the order of the world has been reduced to the aim simply of
inculcating a specifically sapiental life-style. There is a distinct

awareness that the formation of personal character, and the acquisition of the resilience to cope with life's demands and disappointments, is a primary goal of wisdom. The emphasis has shifted towards 'being wise', rather than 'knowing wisdom'.

In a further direction Qoheleth is important in that, unlike the slightly later work of Ben Sira (ca. 170 BCE), he has not felt any necessity to make wisdom conform in any precise fashion to the demands of a written *torah*. The Wisdom of Solomon from the Old Testament Apocrypha appears even more on the fringe of our examination. It marks a stage when Jewish wisdom had come to be deeply influenced by Hellenistic ideas and when many of the earlier wisdom presuppositions no longer served to mould its primary aims and content. It is an attempt at a kind of philosophical discourse, based on the established traditions of wisdom, but which have been utilised to serve a particular aim, more akin to that of Greek philosophy than that of the earliest wisdom. In one major way it marks a certain crisis point for wisdom since the warm embrace that it offers to Greek philosophical ideas and thought represented a serious departure from the essential Jewishness of the earlier wisdom. It represented a quite radical advance upon the teaching of those who had earlier used the concept of wisdom to break out from a national to a universalist frame of thinking.

The Hellenising tendency, which is first noticeable with Qoheleth and Ben Sira, has become a paramount feature in the Wisdom of Solomon. Such a development is intelligible enough in view of the way in which wisdom had served to provide an intellectual foundation for the process whereby Jews became citizens of many nations and lands. Yet eventually it brought about its downfall as a major stream of intellectual life. In any case, by the time of the rise of the Christian Church, a whole new mix of impulses, both philosophical and religious, had made the original distinctiveness of wisdom a less important factor in Jewish life. The roots of this distinctiveness lay far back in the ancient Near East where wisdom offered the most engaging and adventurous of the intellectual fruits born of the innate human desire to understand and master the uncertainties of life.

Wisdom as a Foundation for Theology

From the perspective of the study of the theological significance of the Israelite wisdom tradition a special interest
attaches to its contribution to the intellectual needs of Judaism
as a community dispersed among the nations. The world of the
Jewish dispersion was a world in which Jews had become
largely cut off from the Jerusalem temple, which had provided,
through its combination of cultic and monarchic ideologies, the
source and centre of their intellectual heritage. Life in
dispersion, 'among the nations roundabout', was a world of
liminality. Wisdom's unique contribution was to be found in
the way in which it offered a new, non-monarchic and non-
cultic, framework for concepts concerning the nature and
meaning of the world. Once this came to be combined with an
extensive reminting of the older cultic imagery and terminology, its teaching could be adapted to provide a non-national,
universalistic, world view. Our contention is that, since this is
largely, although not entirely, unique to Israel's wisdom
tradition, it was the distinctive demands of the diaspora
situation which served to shape its development in this way.

All attempts to trace the origin of ideas and to examine their
functioning in specific situations involves a recognition of the
reciprocity between idea and event. Ideas arise to cope with
new situations, but, conversely, the prior existence of such
ideas, at least in a germinal form, is usually necessary for them
to function in a specific context. We are not concerned
therefore to claim that wisdom developed an a-cultic universalistic outlook in order to provide a basis of instruction for Jews
living in dispersion. Rather it is that, because of its distinctive
origins, originally in a relatively confined area of Israelite life,
wisdom provided the tools by which the experience of life in
the Jewish dispersion could be viewed and conceptualised in a
new way.

The promotion of a deepened emphasis upon the inwardness
and spiritual meaning of cultic activity was one way in which
wisdom exercised a powerful influence among the exiles. At the
same time we may claim that the popularity among the sages of
drawing up lists, and of encouraging literacy, also enabled it to
summarise and codify rules of moral conduct. Certainly the

moral demands and dilemmas of life occupied the centre-stage of the post-exilic teachers of wisdom, making it a profoundly ethical body of education and leading to a characteristically sapiental idea of virtue.

Although the consequences of good or bad actions may usually be readily identified, what broader principles determine the 'goodness' and 'badness' of such actions is less easily defined. Attempts to establish universally applicable rules display strong limitations and, understandably, the *torah*-centered morality of the Deuteronomic literature may be said to contain within itself inevitable weaknesses. Certainly it is noteworthy that the strong emphasis set out in Deut. 5–9 upon the necessity for obedience to the *torah* displays a consciousness that, where the will to comply is lacking, the law itself becomes ineffective.

This does not, of course, imply that human societies have had no awareness of codes of conduct concerning what constitutes desirable, or undesirable, activities. Nevertheless codes of written laws do not provide more than a partial, and sometimes misleading guide, to the nature of the ethical standards of a community. Laws are formulated in order to deal with the felt need for regulating the behaviour of persons living together in a shared territory. They are seldom called upon to set out widely applicable principles of behaviour. So it remains true that universally valid formal definitions concerning what is good have never been easy to set out.

The strong sanctions based on the honour, or shame, of a family or clan point us to recognize this,[29] as also does the high importance attached in ancient societies to the ethical associations of such cultic concepts as holiness. What was approved in these communities was, in large measure, a way of life that was conformable to the demands of the deity worshipped by its members. Organized worship therefore played a very substantial role in maintaining the quality of life

---

29. The extensive use by the prophets of the concept of 'shame' (Heb. *bosh*) to signify, not simply humiliation but ruination and catastrophe, amply exemplifies the moral significance attaching to the concept of 'honour'. Cf. J. Pedersen, *Israel. Its Life and Culture*, I–II, (Copenhagen: Branner, 1926), pp. 213–244; M. A. Klopfenstein, *Scham und Schande nach dem Alten Testament*, AT ANT 62, (Zürich: Theologischer Verlag, 1972).

of a community and in regulating the behaviour of its members. All the indications that the Old Testament presents to us point to the recognition that this was so in pre-exilic Israel and Judah. The provision of a system of law, and its enforcement, was at best only partial and beset with serious flaws which undermined its effectiveness. All this is well evidenced from the condemnations of the prophets, but is equally well supported by the frequent injunctions to law-abiding integrity advocated in many early wisdom admonitions, as well as in the Psalter.

While normal community relations prevailed for ancient Israel, and while access to formal worship was uninhibited, such sanctions and norms as it proferred were as adequate to everyday demands as could be expected. Yet it was precisely the liminality of life in exile that called forth a broadening and rethinking of the bases of moral action. Most especially was this necessary because the normal community structure which distinguished between the fellow Israelite 'neighbour' (Heb. *rea'*), the 'resident alien', or 'sojourner', (Heb. *ger* and the 'foreigner' (Heb. *nokhri* could clearly no longer be maintained (cf. Deut. 14:21). The very concepts of community organisation which Israel had inherited became obsolete and inadequate once social existence in the dispersion had become a permanent pattern of life.

Insights gained in a time of liminality had to become permanent features of life. What was needed by Jews living in the dispersion was a thoroughgoing reminting of norms of moral and social conduct on a more universalistic basis than the inherited world-view, focused on family and worship, had provided. This was precisely what wisdom claimed to be able to offer.

Overall we may claim that wisdom became uniquely important to the development of a more universalist ethic and understanding of spirituality among Jews after 587 BCE. This was because it represented a tradition that was non-nationalist (Deuteronomic) and non-cultic (Levitical) in its origin and which was therefore free to develop universalist claims. Furthermore, in such a writer as Qoheleth we begin to encounter serious wrestling with the question of human 'happiness', as an aspect of the concern to focus attention on the life-goals of each individual human being and the relationship of such happiness to virtue.

This should not be taken to mean that the shaping of our present wisdom tradition took place primarily among Jews living in dispersion. On the contrary it appears unlikely that this was the case. Rather it became a matter of prime importance to the rise of post-exilic Judaism that the ideas and practices of those in the dispersion and those who remained in the land should not radically differ. All the indications are that there were many issues of controversy and dissension before a substantial measure of agreement was reached between the two communities. We may go so far as to claim that these issues were, in reality, the most difficult and urgent of all those that had to be resolved if Judaism was to survive after 587 BCE. Had there been a failure to achieve a basis of conduct and commitment recognized by all Jews, whether in Judah or in the dispersion (cf. the comprehensive formula of Dan. 9:7) there would have been two Judaisms. No doubt at times the sectarian pressures that were increasingly felt in Judaism from the beginning of the Hellenistic era tended in such a direction. Yet overall the mainstream of Jewish leadership resisted them, and the contribution of wisdom was that it offered a tradition that was authentically Jewish. At the same time it remained open to acceptance of a wider foundation of truth and morality than was contained in the tradition of instruction exclusively mediated through Moses.

In the broadest spectrum of religious development it must be recognized that wisdom was only one of several influences that served to shape Jewish life after the disasters of 587 BCE. The written Old Testament is itself, in all its breadth, essentially a product of this post-587 era, even though it clearly contains much older material. Judaism emerged as 'the religion of a Book'. Among the many influences that brought this about, wisdom was a very formative one. Eventually the crisis period passed and Judaism, with its split between a community in Judah focused upon the temple of Jerusalem and a larger number of Jews in dispersion, achieved a relatively stable form.

CHAPTER TWO

Wisdom and the World

Gerhard von Rad begins his study of Israelite wisdom by drawing attention to the experiential roots which underlie the human desire for knowledge.[1] Before this, it had already established a place for itself in Mesopotamia and in Egypt. It is true that Egypt had no precise counterpart to the concept of wisdom, although many features of *maat* come close to this, but the similarities of literary forms and a number of basic characteristics have convinced many scholars that pre-exilic Israel drew quite substantially upon written traditions of Egyptian wisdom.[2]

We may regard it as certain also that the former Canaanite city kingdoms of the land which Israel came to rule were also familiar with some elements of a tradition of wisdom.[3] In the

---

1. G. von Rad, *Wisdom in Israel*, ET James D. Martin (London: SCM Press, 1972), p. 4: 'Not only does the outside world as an object stimulate man's desire for knowledge; its movements and reactions affect him and, at the same time subject him to influences. In any event, man must know his way about in the world in which he finds himself in order to be able to hold his own in it.'

2. Cf. E. Würthwein, 'Die Weisheit Ägyptens und das Alte Testament', Wort und Existenz (Göttingen: Vandenhoeck & Ruprecht, 1970), pp. 197–216; G. E. Bryce, *A Legacy of Wisdom. The Egyptian Contribution to the Wisdom of Israel* (Lewisburg: Bucknell University Press, 1979), especially pp. 87ff.

3. In the Ugaritic mythological texts the deity El appears to have been especially associated with wisdom. To what extent this may have been encouraged by a belief that wisdom could comprehend a magical-mantic power is not clear. Undoubtedly some types of wisdom texts took the form of incantations. Cf. H.-P. Müller, 'Magisch-mantisch Weisheit und die Gestalt Daniels', *Ugarit-Forschungen*, 1, 1969, pp. 79–94.

light of these historical considerations the streams of influence which converged to form early Israelite wisdom must be regarded as varied, and drawn from more than one area. The task of tracing them becomes yet more complex when we give full weight to the evidence for the existence of a deeply-rooted tradition of folk-wisdom among the clans that were incorporated into Israel. Although therefore there are good reasons for believing that the court-wisdom that grew up in Israel under the Davidic monarchy received its strongest impulses from Egypt, its precise nature and content can only be reconstructed within inevitable limits. Overall there is no very clear evidence for believing that such wisdom displayed a unified concept of what conduct was demanded of human beings, nor that the collection and promotion of wisdom was developed to serve any one single purpose within the national life. Some aspects of wisdom's teaching indicate that it was encouraged and sponsored within a narrow professional group, reflecting its own specific interests, whereas other features point to a broader, and more widely popular, function.

Wisdom and a Comprehensive World-View

Throughout its growth in Israel two facets of wisdom's public presentation show themselves. These are on the one hand its predilection for forms of artistic, and sometimes witty, saying.[4] Whatever wisdom had to say it wished to say well. Consequently we find that wisdom employed extensive use of verbal imagery in propounding its truths, and was also closely associated with riddles, fables and allegories. In fact some forms of wisdom saying appear primarily to have been formulated in order to express some verbal artistry and wit.

Alongside this there stands the evident fact that, in a broader setting, wisdom had a pragmatic and utilitarian function. It was concerned to educate, and so to enable men and women to improve the quality of their lives and to prepare them to cope with its more painful and difficult demands. It proferred advice that was believed to work when put into practice and to describe reliably and perceptively the way the world is actually

---

4. Cf. J. L. Crenshaw, *Old Testament Wisdom* (London: SCM Press, 1982), pp. 31f.

experienced. Clearly the twofold demands of these aims, to be artistic and to be helpful, did not always coincide. Sometimes we can discern that unpopular truths needed to be cloaked in a garment of humour to make them more acceptable. Accordingly the more intricate aspects of verbal artistry in riddles, and in the use of hyperbole and paranomasia to drive home a particular point, are evident.[5] Conversely artistry has sometimes been sacrificed to accommodate to the requirements of truth and reality.

Neither of these apparent ambitions, however, lead us to conclude that there existed, either in Israel, or in the wider spheres of Mesopotamian or Egyptian life, any single agreed world-view that was embraced by wisdom. It was not a philosophy, and Israelite wisdom did not inherit any such philosophy. Although undoubtedly the later wisdom writers such as Qoheleth and Ben Sira sought to develop more comprehensive all-round perspectives on life, these were essentially a result of their own systematising propensities. Their teachings were based on inherited wisdom teachings and only in this fashion can they be said to have attempted a coherent and consistent view of the world. By this time both writers had received impulses generated by popular Greek philosophy. In any case the work of Qoheleth shows a consistency of attitude and style, rather than being expressive of a truly comprehensive doctrine about life. He urges the adoption of a specific attitude, rather than adherence to a particular creed.

Essentially the most significant of the assumptions of early wisdom were startlingly wide-ranging and open-ended. A measure of distortion arises as soon as some of its most characteristic proverbial sayings and admonitions are elevated to the level of universal truths. Their limited and *ad hoc* nature is evident, so that they are not applicable to every situation, but are to be acted upon only where they are seen to be appropriate.[6]

---

5. For riddles in the Old Testament an excellent survey is provided by J. L. Crenshaw in *Samson. A Secret Betrayed, a Vow Ignored* (Atlanta: John Knox Press, 1978), pp. 99f.

6. Cf. J. G. Williams, *Those Who Ponder Proverbs: Aphoristic Thinking and Biblical Literature* (Sheffield: Almond Press, 1981).

Another feature which affects our understanding of the nature of early Israelite wisdom concerns the extent to which it can be assumed to have been a literary development. It is abundantly clear from its characteristic forms of instruction, the proverb, the fable, the riddle and various types of parable and allegory, that they were originally composed for oral delivery. Their impact is closely bound up with their brevity and aural effect. However, once wisdom began to adapt to literary forms, far more complex and intricate types of word-connection and verbal artistry became possible.[7] At the same time the newer forms of literary wisdom, precisely on account of their more extended structures, tended to lose something of the sharpness that the earlier short spoken sayings had enjoyed. From a theological perspective what was more significant than this loss of auditory effect was the fact that the literary fixation of wisdom promoted the need for greater harmony of content. Once sayings were written down they could be compared and contrasted with each other and more universal truths deduced from them. It is not altogether surprising therefore that from an early period the scribes who were enthused about the pursuit of wisdom appear to have found great delight in the composing of lists.[8]

By the very nature of history it is such collections of literary wisdom that have survived for us to examine. Except where they are now embodied into written anthologies, the older spoken types of wisdom saying are usually only to be found more haphazardly reported in narratives. As in so many aspects of linguistic and intellectual development, the changes incurred by the transition from spoken to written wisdom can

---

7. The significance of the tensions and shifts between oral and written wisdom appear still to lack any very close examination. It may indeed be the case that the pursuit of wisdom encouraged literacy and so much wisdom teaching was written from the outset. However this would appear to sit uneasily with the observation that many of the more overtly artistic features of wisdom belong within the setting of a predominantly oral situation. Aural effect was clearly of great importance to many early wisdom sayings. They were evidently intended to be heard and memorised, rather than recorded and read.

8. Cf. J. Goody, 'What's in a list?' *The Domestication of the Savage Mind* (Cambridge: CUP, 1977), pp. 74–111.

only partially be identified.[9] However it is reasonable for us to make the assumption that, for virtually the entire period in which the Old Testament was in process of formation, oral and written wisdom teaching were carried on side by side. Almost certainly the short sayings of Proverbs 10–29 reflect their origin in oral instruction, whereas the more elaborate artistic structures of Prov. 1–9 reflect a distinctly literary stage of development. Yet the passage from the one to the other was not accomplished at a single stroke and the effects of the transition must have shown themselves only slowly.

Nevertheless the issue of the shift from oral to written wisdom has an important bearing upon our concern with the theology of wisdom, since written preservation undoubtedly contributed greatly to the establishing of normative ideas and concepts. The intellectual demand for comparison and harmonisation of fundamental ideas and perceptions led to a more rounded body of teaching. Moreover, once affirmed in writing, the need became more acute to bring the teaching of wisdom into harmony with the teachings of other streams of Israelite tradition, notably that of the cultus. Once it was available for scrutiny as a text, the teaching of wisdom could be examined from many fresh angles.

We may work on the general assumption therefore that Israelite wisdom began with no single corpus of ideas which formed an integrated philosophy of wisdom. Rather it inherited certain fundamental insights and assumptions which came gradually to be co-ordinated into a more coherent and established form.[10] The literary collection of a corpus of wisdom teaching in itself gave rise to a process of theologising which was central to the very nature of what wisdom purported to be. Isolated truths and perceptions needed to be co-ordinated into a more universal body of truth. The particular theological appeal of wisdom lies in the fact that, of all the

---

9. Cf. W. J. Ong, *Orality and Literacy. The Technologizing of the Word* (London & New York: Methuen, 1982), pp. 78ff.
10. Such a conclusion raises serious doubts therefore whether it is at all worthwhile attempting to identify a particular field of wisdom vocabulary, as R. B. Y. Scott, *The Way of Wisdom in the Old Testament* (New York: Macmillan, 1971), pp. 48ff. Such specific areas of interest were largely dictated by the kind of themes and concerns relating to human conduct which occupied the attention of the sages.

features of Israelite intellectual life, wisdom had most to gain from the adoption of a written form. Writing could be looked upon as a specific skill which bore the hallmark of education and learning on account of its value in communication and commerce. At the same time it promoted reflection and accuracy of expression. Furthermore, as in the spread of literacy in all societies, the acquisition of writing skills invariably carried with it a greatly increased range of vocabulary. As an instrument for the promotion of better and fuller understanding, therefore, it is likely that the pursuit of literacy enjoyed a high priority among the wise. Accordingly the categories of 'wise man' and 'scribe' must frequently have overlapped.

Most imposing of the assumptions of early wisdom in Egypt, Mesopotamia and Israel appears to have been a note of confidence concerning human ability to perceive and grasp the nature of reality. The world is taken to be in actuality what it appears to be to the eye of the skilled observer. Observation of persons and things, therefore takes pride of place among the methods by which wisdom is to be obtained. Supporting this there is evident a deep conviction that an order pervades all things and that it is the dictates of wisdom that shape and uphold this order.[11] From the perspective of modern critical concern to uncover the basic ideas of wisdom this search for order appears as the most pervasive of all its assumptions. Wisdom affirms that a planned and coherent order determines the relationships between all things. That such an order may not be readily apparent required that it be searched for behind and beneath the appearance of things. This entailed the belief that the truths of wisdom could sometimes be hidden and unnoticed by the casual observer. In turn this inevitably led to the conviction that a major distinction existed between the shrewd observer and the fool.

The natural world, the realm of human conduct, and the organizational structures of human society, were all believed to lie within this one sustaining order of wisdom that had been

---

11. In Egypt this order was the prime feature of the study of Maat. Cf. A. Volten, 'Der Begriff der Maat in den Ägyptischen Weisheitstexten', *Les sagesses du Proche-Orient Ancien* (Paris: Presses Universitaires de France, 1963), pp. 73–99.

laid down at the creation of the universe. In pursuance of this belief the theme of creation, and the wisdom of the Creator, were subjects of prime importance to the sages. Alongside this went the belief that closely similar patterns could be observed in the varied operations of natural phenomena. Consistency, regularity and similarity were taken to be important clues to finding out about the inner structure of life.[12] Likeness was taken to be more than a mark of apparent harmony. It was taken to be the visible sign of an underlying connection and so could serve as evidence of a designed symmetry in the world. It is not surprising therefore to find that in Israel the didactic form of the *mashal* (= proverb) points us back to an awareness of *likeness* between things.[13]

So far as Israelite religious thought was concerned the basic assumptions of wisdom could be adapted to fit well into a monotheistic strain of religion. Belief in the oneness of God coincided conveniently well with belief in the essential oneness of the world.[14]

Since wisdom shared these basic assumptions concerning the possibility of human knowledge, but lacked any all-inclusive philosophy, then it could change and adapt to various environments and be applied in more than one way. Although therefore it has been a matter of considerable concern to scholarship to seek to trace the effect upon wisdom of its national incorporation into the life of Israel, it is hard to see that such a process would have entailed any major difficulty.

---

12. It is noteworthy in this regard that the perceptions of divine presence and activity by the wise appear to have been of a very different order from those of the authors of popular cult-legends. Among the latter it was the unusual phenomenon which signified a 'sign' that a divine movement was in process. For the wise, however, it appears predominantly that it was the observed pattern of order and regularity that signified that the 'wise' hand of God was present.

13. It remains very indeterminate in many wisdom sayings how far likeness is taken to be a merely external characteristic which may hide fundamental differences, and how far a more genuine connection was thought to exist. So in the numerical sayings of Prov. 30:15–33 it is important that the shrewd listener/reader should be able to spot the connections.

14. The most striking instance where the claim that the wisdom displayed in the oneness of the world points to a single Creator, is in Isa. 40:13–14. The prophet would appear consciously to be repudiating the widespread religious belief that there existed a skilled Craftsman-Counsellor among the gods.

Wisdom was neither more nor less acceptable to Israelite thought than were other aspects of human activity, social organization and intellectual aspiration. Ancient Near Eastern cultus, and its close association with many varied aspects of mythology, all showed themselves capable of being moulded and adapted into an Israelite form. There are no major reasons for thinking that wisdom proved any more recalcitrant to such a process than did the many varied rites of animal sacrifice.

The theological consequences of the shifts that were occasioned for wisdom by its acceptance into Israelite life, and especially into the Jerusalem court of the pre-exilic period, need not have been all that extensive in their first stages. In general it may be argued that wisdom was no more and no less a desirable item of intellectual food for Israel to swallow, than were the basic assumptions and images of ancient Near Eastern cultus and mythology.

Wisdom and Worship

There are no fundamental reasons for thinking that the pursuit of wisdom, in Egypt, Mesopotamia or Israel, was the particular province of a priestly class. Rather the opposite appears to have been the case so that wisdom was not pursued in any close relation to the cultus, even though the skills of priestly ministry may have been looked upon as one of the many-sided manifestations of wisdom.[15] This is of importance since there are many indications that, as a general practice, the activities of the cult were simply accepted by the sages as a given part of life. Wisdom was not by its nature anti-cultic in its stance, nor yet intentionally pro-cultic. That men and women participated in activities of worship and that all life was surrounded by activities of the cult was simply taken for granted. At most we might be inclined to conclude that wisdom was a-cultic in that it neither wished to affirm, nor deny, the efficacy of ritual activity and the reality of communion with the divine world through rites of worship.

Cf. R. N. Whybray, *The Heavenly Counsellor in Isaiah xl 13–14*, SOTS Monographs 1 (Cambridge: CUP, 1971).
15. The subject is examined in detail by L. G. Perdue, *Wisdom and Cult*, SBLDS 30 (Missoula, MT: Scholars Press, 1977).

However, certain factors meant that, in the course of time, the teachings of the wise and the teachings of the cultus were likely to come into conflict. Most of all this was so because cultus surrounded the whole of life and provided it with a basic set of norms and images.[16]

In the first instance it is evident that, for the earliest forms of Israelite society, the entire perception of time was controlled by the cultus.[17] Time was seasonal time, marked at intervals of the calendar by the celebration of festivals which were themselves responses to the cultivation of the land. The coming of the spring and autumn rains and the aridity of the hot period of high summer, marked times when crops were in their various stages of growth and were all embodied into a cultic calendar. The very possibility of the continuance of life was inseparably bound up with the regularity of the passage of the seasons. Accordingly the traditions concerning the ending of the Great Flood celebrate this event by the divine promise of an orderly maintenance of the seasons (Gen. 9:8–17).

Alongside these agricultural seasons the movements of the heavenly bodies also belonged to the perception of time and its passing (cf. Gen. 1:14). Time therefore was a primary manifestation of the order in life, so much so that the marking of the passage of time and the changing of the seasons was primary to the performance of all cultus.

All that transpired between the divine and human worlds was a series of actions performed at the proper times, and designed to make these transition periods beneficial to human beings. Consequently the rituals the cultus enjoined were related to these seasonal transitions and were intended to respond to them. At this basic level their performance was aimed at promoting a smooth passage for human beings

---

16. Cf. H.-J Kraus, *Worship in Israel. A Cultic History of the Old Testament*, ET G. Buswell (Oxford: B.H. Blackwell, 1966), p. 23: 'It is often scarcely conceivable how the institutions and regulations of Israel are overlooked or neglected in the study of the history of worship.' The importance of the world-view presupposed and implied by the cultus and its symbolism is well described in F. Gorman, Jr. *The Ideology of Ritual. Space, Time and Status in the Priestly Theology*, JSOTSupp 91 (Sheffield: Sheffield Academic Press, 1990).
17. Cf. Gorman, *op. cit*, pp. 33ff.; J. Pedersen, *Israel 1–11*, pp. 487ff., especially p. 490: 'The conceptions of time and space are uniform; in both

through these seasonal changes. Accordingly the origins of all ancient cultus are to be sought in the concern to maintain a stable order of life and society. Ritual, cultic symbolism and prayer were engaged in a process of upholding a divinely established world order.

It is clear therefore that a potential basis for a conflict of ideas between cultus and wisdom existed because wisdom sought to identify the nature of the order that existed in the world along different lines from those upheld by the cultus. In the earliest period it is likely that the sages simply accepted, without necessarily endorsing, the conception of time upheld by the cultus with its seasonal festivals. Time was part of a mysterious order, controlled and revealed by the movements of the sun and moon, to which human beings had to submit. Yet such an external and cyclic view of time left too little room for the human, life-centered, awareness of time which noted the immense variety of human activities, moods and experiences which determined the individual's valuation of it.

Time, in its cultic presentation, could appear as fatalistic, overbearing and burdensome. Human beings had to submit to the manifestation of a pre-ordained pattern of time reflecting an annual seasonal cycle of life, death and rebirth. Certainly, in reflecting upon the divine control of time the psalmist could find in it a rather overpowering reality:

> You sweep men away; they are like a dream,
>   like grass which is renewed in the morning:
> in the morning it flourishes and is renewed;
>   in the evening it fades and withers.
>   Ps. 90:5–6

Over against the centrality of the seasonal symbolism of time in the cultus, it is noteworthy that the teaching of wisdom focused attention on the orderliness of the universe in a much more individualistic and private manner. This is already evident in the formulation of Ps. 104, with its heavy influence from wisdom:

---

cases it is a question of wholes which are not sharply outlined, but determined by their character and quality.'

Thou hast made the moon to mark the seasons:
    the sun knows its time for setting.
Thou makest darkness and it is night,
    when all the beasts of the forest creep forth.

. . .

Man goes forth to his work
    and to his labour until the evening.

                                        Ps. 104:19–23

Over against the great emphasis upon the cultic seasonal marking and symbolising of time it is striking that Old Testament wisdom's fullest disquisition on the subject comes from Qoheleth in the late third century BCE.:

A time to be born, and a time to die;
a time to plant, and a time to pluck up what is planted;
a time to kill, and a time to heal;
a time to break down, and a time to build up;
a time to weep, and a time to laugh;
a time to mourn, and a time to dance;
a time to throw away stones, and a time to gather stones together;
a time to embrace, and a time to refrain from embracing;
a time to seek, and a time to lose;
a time to keep, and a time to throw away;
a time to tear, and a time to sew;
a time to keep silence, and a time to speak;
a time to love, and a time to hate;
a time for war, and a time for peace.
What ultimate gain (Heb. *yithron* = gain, reward) has the worker
    from his toil?

                                        Qoh. 3:2–9

Undoubtedly there has been a conscious striving in this poem for artistic balance and effect, obtained by the setting up of contrasts. Certainly too we may regard it as a personal and individual reflection on the meaning of time by Qoheleth, although he may well have utilised older prototypes for such a composition.[18] Nevertheless it is surprising how completely

---

18. The poem has justifiably elicited a great deal of discussion. Cf. J. L. Crenshaw, *Ecclesiastes*, OTL (London: SCM Press, 1989), pp. 91–100; G. Ogden, *Qoheleth* (Sheffield: The Almond Press, 1989), pp. 51ff. ; M. V.

this composition has succeeded in humanising the perception of time. Its overall purpose, as noted in v.9, is to discern what is the 'gain' (Heb. *yithron* = 'accrued gain', 'life purpose', and hence 'goal', 'meaning').[19] No longer is it the seasonal cycle of nature, the festivals of the cultus, nor yet the movement of the heavenly bodies that controls the passage and awareness of time. Rather time is first and foremost characterised by the life-span of each individual, as this is affirmed by the parameters set in the opening line: there is a time to be born and a time to die. Thereafter the passage of time is perceived as a series of life-opportunities to which each human being responds freely and creatively according to the needs and dictates of the moment. It is presented in terms of humanly experienced time which serves as a vehicle for the expression of individual emotions, powers and achievements.[20]

Overall Qoheleth comes close to expressing an existential understanding of time which recognizes its overwhelming importance to each individual and seeks to find in the light and shade of daily life a pattern and order. For all the sombre tones of the intense interest in the theme of death and its inevitability which Qoheleth displays, his understanding of this, like his understanding of time, stands at a very considerable distance from the more fatalistic and deterministic notions of human history which characterised apocalyptic and the cultic calendars from which it drew.

We have only to reflect upon the exaggerated way in which the cultic understanding of time has been magnified in the Book of Jubilees into becoming a key by which to unlock the mysteries of the whole of human history to recognize how differently the subject is presented by Qoheleth. Nor should we suppose that Qoheleth is reacting in a purely personal fashion to the subject, since his reflections stand at the head of

---

Fox, *Qoheleth and His Contradictions* (Sheffield: Sheffield Academic Press, 1989), pp. 191–193.

19. For this meaning of the Hebrew *yithron* cf. G. Ogden, *op. cit.*, pp. 27ff.

20. Seen in this light the attempt of G. von Rad, *Wisdom in Israel*, pp. 138f. to link Qoheleth's disquisition on time with the apocalyptic notion of fixed ages and the division of all human history into pre-ordained periods appears to be wholly misdirected. The former is positive and strongly focused upon human individuality and freedom. Conversely the latter places each

an older tradition of wisdom teaching which regarded the individual's life-span as the most fundamental unit of time, rather than the life-death-life cycle of the cultic year. We may reasonably conclude therefore that, in its desire to incorporate the experience of time into the pattern of cosmic order, wisdom pointed in a very different direction from the earlier traditions inherited from the cultus.

The Realm of Sacred Space

If wisdom pointed in the direction of humanising and de-mythologising the awareness of time, then just as fully and firmly did it lead towards a major series of changes in the conceptualisation of space. When we examine the ways in which territory and space are perceived in early Israel, it is clear that, in this area also, the symbolism of the cultus provided the central core of images and ideas. Cosmology was an intellectual construct which conveyed a cult-oriented conception of order in the universe.[21]

The inhabited world was a circle, or more truly a series of circles, in which the temple stood at the centre. This was the 'Holy Mountain'—the sacred point of meeting between the divine and human worlds (Pss. 46, 48, 73). This holy mountain was the representative focal point for the entire territory which Israel inhabited (cf. Exod. 15:17).[22] From this centre the

---

individual under the control of pre-ordained purposes in which he, or she, is wholly passive.

21. The subject is dealt with in R. L. Cohn, *The Shape of Sacred Space. Four Biblical Studies*, AARSR 23 (Chico, CA: Scholars Press, 1981), pp. 25ff. I am particularly indebted to Cohn's study for drawing my attention to the work of Victor Turner and its understanding of the idea of liminality as a basic condition for encouraging intellectual development and change. The applicability of Cohn's (and Turner's) insights into several of the most striking features of the concepts and terminology of Israelite wisdom has encouraged me to take further researches along these lines. What has been lacking hitherto has been an adequate appreciation of the social context in which the concepts and aims of Israelite-Jewish wisdom could function effectively.

22. Cf. R. J. Clifford, *The Cosmic Mountain in Canaan and the Old Testament*, Harvard Semitic Monographs 4, (Cambridge, Mass. : Harvard UP, 1972), 98ff.; F. Stolz, *Strukturen und Figuren im Kult von Jerusalem*, BZAW 118 (Berlin: de Gruyter, 1970), pp. 149ff. The subject was earlier examined by me in *God and Temple. The Idea of the Divine Dwelling-place in the Old Testament* (Oxford: B. H. Blackwell, 1965), pp. 1ff. Cf. also Ben C.

vitality and healing power of the cultus flowed out, as is most clearly expressed in the Ezekiel Reconstruction Programme (Ezek. 40–48):

> Then he brought me back to the door of the temple; and behold, water was issuing from below the threshold of the temple toward the east (for the temple faced east); and the water was flowing down from below the south end of the threshold of the temple, south of the altar
>
> . . .
>
> And wherever the river goes every living creature which swarms will live, and there will be very many fish; for this water goes there, that the waters of the sea may become fresh; so everything will live where the river goes
>
> . . .
>
> And on the banks, on both sides of the river, there will grow all kinds of trees for food. Their leaves will not wither nor their fruit fail, but they will bear fresh fruit every month, because the water for them flows from the sanctuary. Their fruit will be for food, and their leaves for healing.
>
> Ezek. 47:1–12

No doubt this prophetic vision is heavily stylised and simplified, but the central feature is that space and territory are presented in terms of a cultic symbolism which interpreted their value as a space for human activity by means of cultic concepts and imagery. There existed a centre where the temple stood and a periphery which was dependent upon this centre for its vitality and suitability for habitation.

Further consequences of this conceptualisation of space in terms of the cultus and its mythology are to be seen in the manner in which it determined ideas of cleanness and uncleanness. A most striking instance of this is to be seen in the threat expressed by Amos to the priest Amaziah intimating that he would be taken off into exile:

Ollenburger, *Zion The City of the Great King*, JSOTSupp 41 (Sheffield: Sheffield Academic Press, 1987), pp. 66ff.; H.-J. Kraus, *op. cit.*, pp. 201ff.

> . . . you yourself shall die in an unclean land,
> and Israel shall surely go into exile
>   away from its land.
>
>   Amos 7:17

To be compelled to live at a distance from active participation in the cultus was to be forced to live without the cleansing and healing effect of its rituals.

Such prophetic warnings, which still find echoes later in the exilic prophets Jeremiah and Ezekiel, reveal the extent to which, for early Israel, all space was conceived in terms of sacred space. Geography itself was a highly stylised geography in which the vitality of the holy place stood at the centre and on the periphery there existed the mysterious and threatening spaces of desert and darkness.[23] Territory itself had to be rendered clean and holy by the presentation of appropriate gifts to its divine Lord. In the background the ever-threatening power of 'The Mighty Waters' existed as a warning that the reality of creation could only be secured by the repeated re-creative activities of the cultus.[24]

It is especially in its willingness and ability to develop a conceptual world of space and time that dispensed with these deeply rooted cultic notions and symbols that marked out wisdom as a fresh intellectual discipline. The origins of this different approach to these broad intellectual constructs lie in the nature of wisdom's inherited assumptions. Nevertheless it is clear that they were especially well suited to the needs of Israelites who had to fashion a life for themselves outside the established boundaries of a national territory. The primary

---

23. Besides the study of R. L. Cohn noted above, pp. 7ff. cf. also S. Talmon, 'The "Desert Motif" in the Bible and in Qumran Literature', *Biblical Motifs. Origins and Transformations*, ed. A. Altmann, Studies and Texts Vol. III (Cambridge, Mass.: Harvard Univ. Press, 1966), pp. 31–63; L. I. J. Stadelman, SJ, *The Hebrew Conception of the World. A Philological and Literary Study*, Analecta Biblica 39 (Rome: Pontinfical Institute Press, 1970), *passim*. Walter Harrelson, 'The Significance of Cosmology in the Ancient Near East', *Translating and Understanding the Old Testament. Essays in Honor of H. G. May*, eds. H. T. Frank and W. L. Reed (New York–Nashville: Abingdon Press, 1970), pp. 237–252.
24. For the Canaanite background to such 'Conflict Mythology' see now John Day, *God's Conflict with the Dragon and the Sea: Echoes of Canaanite Myth in the Old Testament*, UCOP 35 (Cambridge: CUP, 1985).

issue was how could it be that Israel should not 'die' in an unclean land? The very idea of exile was perceived as a form of uncleanness that must inevitably lead to death. To live at a distance from active participation in the cultus was not simply a matter of being deprived of its stimulus and re-assurance. It was separation from the cohesive centre of the concepts and symbolism by which the experienced world was rendered friendly and intelligible. The cultus, in ancient Israel as in the ancient Near East generally, provided the frame of reference by which the everyday world, with its many contrasting faces, was provided with a conceptual shape and character.

We may accept that already in pre-exilic Israel the court scribes who urged the pursuit of wisdom had learnt to describe the spatial world in ways that leaned in a distinctive direction away from the ideas maintained by the cultus. Most notably in Ps. 104, which displays strong wisdom influence, do we find a picture of earth as a territory in which all is held together harmoniously and beneficently by the mysterious design of wisdom. Each part of the world, both that which is inhabited and that which lies beyond the known spaces where humans live, is seen as part of a divinely designed cosmos. Distinctions between 'clean' and 'unclean' no longer convey any meaningful significance. The psalmist has quite evidently gone out of his way to stress that even the most traditonally threatening feature of the world—the Great Deep (Heb. *mayyim rabbim*)—is in truth part of the beneficent cosmic order:[25]

> O Lord, how manifold are thy works!
> In wisdom you have made them all;
> the earth is full of your creatures.
> Over there lies the sea, great and wide,
> which teems with innumerable things,
> living things both small and great.
> There go the ships,
> and Leviathan which your made to play in it.
> Ps. 104:24–26

The date of origin of Ps. 104 is far from certain, but it may be

---

25. The mythical understanding of the sea in ancient Israel in the light of its ancient Near Eastern background is fully explored in O. Kaiser, *Die*

held to express a picture of world order which has been
strongly influenced by wisdom at an early stage. That it even
reflects strong Egyptian influence, as was at one time
maintained, cannot be ruled out.

Most strikingly in the divine speeches in Job 38–41, which
bring to a close Job's spiritual and physical ordeal, we find a de-
sacralising of the notion of sacred space.[26] All space is viewed as
cosmos—a realm of designed order and beneficence—even
where neither the eye nor intellect of human beings can trace
the full operation of its wonders. The strongest possible
affirmation is given that such order exists and that all the
created sphere of the natural world conforms to the plans and
intentions of its divine Creator. If there is mystery and disorder
it lies, not in the creation itself, but in the weak and imperfect
manner by which the creaturely human eye and heart respond
to this order. In a celebrated reflection upon animal behaviour
in the natural world, even the disorderly conduct of the ostrich
is viewed as a departure from the innate wisdom with which she
was endowed (Job 39:13–18). Her apparently neglectful
treatment of her young, which seems to run counter to the
dictates of wisdom, is not accepted as a defect in the original
scheme of things but as a negligent departure from it.

In a remarkable way wisdom has provided a central core of
assumptions and a newness of attitude that has set aside many
of the basic tenets of the mythological world-view propagated
in the older forms of Israelite cultus. In consequence the strong
prevalence in the cult of the theme of conflict, and the quasi-
physical imbuing of space and territory with ideas of life and
death, purity and uncleanness, have been totally transformed.[27] The extent to which a substantial measure of wisdom
influence has been felt in the fashioning of the Priestly Creation

---

mythische Bedeutung des Meeres in Ägypten, Ugarit und Israel, BZAW 78
(Berlin: A. Töpelmann, 1959).

26. Cf. N. C. Habel, *The Book of Job. A Commentary* (London: SCM Press,
1985), especially pp. 517ff.

27. It is important in this regard to note the contribution of the work of Mary
Douglas, *Purity and Danger. An Analysis of the Concepts of Pollution and
Taboo* (London: Routledge and Kegan Paul, 1966); cf. also her study *Natural
Symbols. Explorations in Cosmology* (New York: Pantheon Books, 1970).

Narrative of Gen. 1:1–2.4a may be variously estimated.[28] On the understanding set forth here it was very considerable. Most particularly we should note the complete lack of any reflection on any basic distinctions in the created order between 'clean' and 'unclean', and between the 'holy' and the 'profane'. Instead the repeated affirmation is made that all the creation is 'good' (Gen. 1:3, 4, 10 etc.). It is somewhat paradoxical therefore that this narrative has acquired the label 'Priestly' when in it the older cultic ideas and imagery have been submitted to such extensive revaluation.

It is perfectly conceivable that all these shifts would have manifested themselves in the development of the Old Testament wisdom tradition in any case, without the experience of exile to lend to them an added stimulus. Nevertheless, so marked is the manner in which wisdom has provided a different framework for ideas of space and time from those which originated in the cultus, that it is hard not to believe that a very special impetus has occasioned this. Wisdom's concepts and images of the physical world accord with a broader, more secular, and more universal portrayal of it than that which the cultus offered. So far is this true that it appears that they have been greatly fostered by their usefulness to Israel's condition of liminality in the world of diaspora. Perhaps it is possible to place too much emphasis upon the diaspora in this regard, for it appears likely that conditions in Judah in the Persian era did not differ greatly from the mixed and uncertain world that Jews found further afield from their homeland.[29]

For the cultus, Israel's existence as a nation, its occupation of a specific territory, and its ability to ward off the threatening powers of darkness and uncleanness, all formed part of one single continuum. This belonged within a comprehensive mythological world-view which was focused on the institutions and rituals of the cultus.[30] A whole process of revaluing and re-

28. Cf. C. Westermann, *Genesis 1–11*, ET J. J. Scullion (London: SPCK, 1984), p. 92.

29. Cf. P. R. Ackroyd, 'The Jewish Community in Palestine in the Persian Period', *The Cambridge History of Judaism, Vol. I. The Persian Period*, eds. W. D. Davies & L. Finkelstein (Cambridge: CUP, 1984), pp. 130–161.

30. Cf. Mary Douglas, 'The Healing Rite', *Implicit Meanings. Essays in Anthropology* (London: Routledge & Kegan Paul, 1975), p. 150: 'No one has done more than Levi-Strauss to display the interlocking categories of culture.

imaging the natural order of life, space and time was necessary
if the Jews of the the dispersion were not to suffer the inevitable
death of their living 'in an unclean land'.

The Beginning of Wisdom

A number of valuable studies have followed upon the
recognition that for Jews to have survived in the new and
hostile world of exile *a* primary—we should certainly say *the*
primary—obstacle lay in the separation from the Jerusalem
temple and its cultus. A wealth of material, especially in the
prophetic books of Jeremiah and Ezekiel, reveal how intensely
the deprivation from cultus was felt and how difficult was the
idea to accept that God himself had given command for the
destruction of his own sanctuary. (cf. Jer. 7; Ezek. 9).[31] The
whole Zion-centredness of Israelite worship appeared to have
been discredited at a single stroke.

It is evident that the crisis engendered by this situation was
met by the elaboration of a strong prophetic apologetic. On the
one hand this focused attention on the long history of idolatry
evident in practices pursued by the inhabitants of Jerusalem,
and even rejected categorically some aspects of the old temple
cultus (cf. Ezek. 8:1–18; Jer. 7:30). On the other hand it led to
the emergence of a radical prophetic eschatology which looked
forward to the building of a new and purified temple (Ezek. 40–
48).

However neither of these prophetic resolutions of the
difficulty created by the cessation of the worship of the
Jerusalem temple could properly deal with the question of how
Israel was to live in the period of the 'in between' time. Only
the vaguest of formulae emerged to suggest that God had made
special provision for his people in this period of liminality until
the temple cultus should be restored (cf. Ezek. 11:16; Jer.
29:10–14. The affirmation of 1 Kgs. 8:45 is also of signifi-

These constitute a public symbolic system which is available to everyone to
draw upon who is a member of the culture. He shows how they are based
upon basic social categories and how they schematise all the material aspects
of life into patterns of meaning.'
31. Cf. now particularly R. W. Klein, *Israel in Exile. A Theological
Interpretation*, Overtures to Biblical Theology (Philadelphia: Fortress Press,
1979), pp. 44ff.

cance). The deep awareness of the 'uncleanness' of life in exile is fully reflected in the promise of the special ritual and spiritual act of 'cleansing' that God would bring for his people before they could be re-established in their own land once again (Ezek. 36:25–27).

It is in the wisdom literature that we find a fruitful outworking of a carefully thought out process entailing the revaluing of fundamental cultic concepts. This becomes most evident in the almost complete eclipse in the Book of Proverbs of the idea of holiness, the concept which had most fully enshrined the notion that Israel was a nation specially chosen and blessed by God (cf. most especially Exod. 19:5–6; Deut. 7:6).[32] In the legislative pronouncements of the Holiness Code (Lev. 17–26) this concept of holiness becomes the fundamental principle which determines and controls Israel's relationship to God.

It is undoubtedly the case that in this Holiness Code, which itself achieved its written form in the post-587 BCE period, the idea of holiness has undergone a degree of moralisation and spiritualisation. In it the more physical aspects of the concept have been modified, but they have not been removed altogether. Holiness remains a concept inseparably related to the practise of the cultus. Without the performance of ritual and the proper respect for the focal centre of holiness in the temple, the whole concept would have been emptied of its primary meaning. We should not be surprised therefore to find that the vocabulary of holiness has only a very marginal role to play in the admonitions of Proverbs:

> It is a snare for a person to say rashly,
>   'It is holy',
> and to seek how to fulfil these words afterwards.[33]
>   Prov. 20:25

In this saying the declaration that something is 'holy' refers

---

32. Cf. now J. G. Gammie, *Holiness in Israel*, Overtures to Biblical Theology (Minneapolis: Augsburg Fortress, 1990), esp. pp. 125ff.; H.-P. Müller, *TWAT*, Bd.II, 589–609.

33. The text is not wholly clear, but this is how McKane, *Proverbs*, pp. 242, 538, understands the saying. The vow is made first (to impress the hearers) and ways of fulfilling it are only thought about later.

to the making of a vow, otherwise the notion of holiness is kept exclusively for the divine realm (Prov. 9:10; 30:3). Even Qoheleth, who enjoins an attitude of great respect and circumspection towards the cultus and its duties, views this almost wholly as a matter of personal integrity and self-respect (Qoh. 5:1–6). It is in no way a quasi-physical participation in a life-giving source of strength and power. The emphasis is more or less completely focused upon the attitude of the citizen to the conventions of worship, not upon the life-enhancing virtues of temple ritual.

We may confine our attention to two basic concepts which figure prominently in the Book of Proverbs, but which clearly had a prominent earlier history as part of the vocabulary of worship. If we ask the question how the sages came to describe a supremely virtuous attitude of life, then the answer is given very clearly. It is a pattern of life moulded, shaped and guided by 'the fear of the Lord' (*yir'at YHWH*).[34] Contrastingly, when we enquire about the nature of evil and the wrongness, or harmful nature, of specific types of activity, then the favoured term used by the sages is 'abomination' (Heb. *to'ebhah*).[35]

Already in the admonitions of Prov.10–29 the phrase 'the fear of the Lord' shows itself as a comprehensive description of the way of life, and the appropriate attitude of mind, which the wisdom teachers wished to inculcate:

> The fear of the Lord is a fountain of life
>   providing escape from the snares of death.
>   Prov. 14:27
> A little with the fear of the Lord
>   is better than great wealth and trouble with it.
>   Prov. 15:16

---

34. For the importance of this concept in the wisdom teaching see especially, J. Becker, *Gottesfurcht im Alten Testament*, Analecta Biblica 25 (Rome: Pontifical Institute, 1965); H. F. Fuhs, *TWAT*, Bd. III, 869–893; L. Derousseaux, *La crainte de dieu dans l'ancien testament*, Lectio Divina 63 (Paris: Editions du Cerf, 1970), pp. 102ff. Derousseaux fails to bring out as clearly as does Becker the prominent and distinctive use of the concept in the wisdom tradition; see also J. Haspecker, *Gottesfurcht bei Jesus Sirach*, Analecta Biblica 30 (Rome: Pontifical Institute Press, 1967).
35. Cf. E. Gerstenberger, *THAT*, II, 1051–1055.

The fear of the Lord is instruction in wisdom,
and humility takes precedence over honour.
                              Prov. 15:33
By loyalty and constancy iniquity is atoned for,
and by the fear of the Lord a man avoids harm.
                              Prov. 16:6
The fear of the Lord leads to life;
and the person who possesses it will rest content;
unvisited by harm.
                              Prov. 19:23
The reward for humility and the fear of the Lord
is riches and honour and life.
          Prov. 22:4 (cf. also Prov. 23:27; 24:21; 28:5, 14; 31:30).

However, when we turn to the broader statements regarding
the nature, desirability and rewards of wisdom which are to be
found in the introductory poems of Prov. 1–9 the primacy of
'the fear of the Lord' is still further declared. It is the supreme
virtue, which is to be encouraged, sought after and maintained
by everyone who desires a good life. It is the platform upon
which the life of virtue rests. It is an attitude of mind, a respect
for the role of piety and faith, and also a strong determination
to 'do the right thing', even when it may be costly and difficult
to do so.

The fear of the Lord is the beginning of wisdom
and the knowledge of the Holy One is insight.
                              Prov. 9:10
The fear of the Lord is the beginning of knowledge;
fools despise wisdom and instruction.
                              Prov. 1:7

The reason why such fools behave badly and refuse the
sages' instruction is then further elaborated:

Because they hated knowledge
and did not choose the fear of the Lord,
would have none of my counsel,
and despised all my reproof.
Therefore they shall eat the fruit of their way
and be sated with their own schemes.
                              Prov. 1:29–31

Further admonitions concerning the primacy of the fear of

the Lord as the springboard for right conduct are to be found in Prov. 2:5–8; 3:7, 11, 12, 26. However, in spite of the great attention to this formulation by the sages, there can be no doubt that its origins lay in the cultus.[36] It described in a purely matter of fact way one who participated in the worship of the deity known as the Lord (Yahweh). It focused attention upon the physical act of sharing in the worship of this God and of addressing prayer in this name.

The wisdom teachers, however, have completely transformed its meaning, in the first instance by giving to it a strong psychological character. In their understanding it refers to an inner disposition and attitude of the mind which the person who maintains it retains permanently and applies to all situations. It affects all aspects of daily life and has lost most of its more specific and external connotation, of describing physical participation in an act of worship. Undoubtedly the person who nurtures this attitude of mind is expected to be such a worshipper, but the consequences of doing so are far reaching and affect all areas of conduct. It represents a desire to please the God Yahweh in all things and to give respect to the divine order of social and moral life, according this the highest possible priority. It establishes the ground in which the virtuous life may grow.

The argument of the foregoing sketch of the manner in which the Israelite wisdom tradition developed a comprehensive world-view is built upon three fundamental perceptions. The first of these concerns the formal recognition that the sages who collected and promoted the teaching of wisdom were not members of the cultic institutions of the nation and looked outside of this for their understanding of reality. They were not opposed to the cult, yet neither did they see themselves as its propagandists and defenders. At times they could be strongly affirmative of its value, and at others they viewed it critically and rather distantly. This attitude simply reflected the much older attitude of the various streams of wisdom development that had their roots in the ancient Near East.

However, such an attitude to the cultus on the part of the sages was not one that could continue indefinitely, without

---

36. Cf. J. Becker, *op. cit.*, pp. 210ff.

substantial modification. The cult established through its imagery and mythology the broad outlines of a cosmology and it laid down the lines of demarcation between what was good and beneficial and what was harmful and threatening. Consequently the cult, with its associated mythology, were not separate and superficial features of daily life. They established the norms of understanding by which daily life was governed and which controlled its activities. Concepts of goodness and badness were essentially determined by the cult with its language of holiness and cleanness.

Initially wisdom simply inherited such a world-view and the teachers of it did not consciously strive to present a clearly defined alternative. However, because they started from a different set of perceptions these teachers of wisdom came to move sharply away from these traditional concepts and images. They developed a new, and distinctive, cosmology, which lacked any very strong mythological basis and they sought to lay down new concepts of virtue and goodness. The virtues of the cultus were presented as merely relative virtues, subordinate to higher aims and goals than the quasi-physical and mechanical assurances that the cult could offer.

This 'alternative' world-view of the sages, with its distinctive insights into the nature of virtue and goodness, might well have remained the intellectual property of relatively small and elitist groups within Judaism. It utilised a tradition and vocabulary which those initiated into the goals of wisdom could easily recognise.

Yet the course of Israel's turbulent history decreed otherwise, since at a major time of national disaster, the temple of Jerusalem was destroyed and its priesthood largely dispersed. The loss of the physical centre was more easily sustained than the loss of the larger world of imagery and ideas which the temple had nurtured. The whole intellectual underpinning of faith had been taken away with the temple's destruction. It then became the major contribution of wisdom to have provided for Judaism, both for those Jews who were forced to build a new life for themselves in diaspora as well as those who had to come to terms with re-establishing life in Judah itself, a new world-view.

This utilised the inherited insights of wisdom, but consciously set them up as representing more primary and fundamental concepts by which the nature of reality could be grasped, than the older cultic symbolism and mythology. Wisdom strove to provide a more universal, and more comprehensively basic, picture of the world and its demands than the now obsolete cultic world-view had provided. The situation of liminality created by the destruction of Jerusalem's temple in 587 and the experience of exile brought about the conditions in which a fresh searching after the foundations of truth could be undertaken.

CHAPTER THREE

Wisdom and Health

In Prov. 3:8 the diligent pupil who listens to the wise teacher, and responds to his teaching by fearing and trusting God with a wholehearted commitment, is assured:

> It will be health to your flesh[1]
> and vitality to your body.
>
> Prov: 3:8

We could readily be forgiven for assuming that this was meant in a broad, and essentially metaphorical, way as an assurance that the follower of the dictates of wisdom would enjoy a full and happy life, a promise that the wisdom teachers felt generally able to give. There are ample reasons, however, for recognising that this assurance was intended to be taken literally and that it represents one instance of a widely made affirmation that the path of wisdom was one that could be expected to lead to health and long life.

The full extent of this connection between wisdom and health is to be seen in the second century BC, in the writing of Ben Sira, where he bids his readers give honour and praise to the physician and pharmacist whose skills are given to human kind by God in order to bring healing and relief to those

---

1. The Hebrew is obscure and this rendering follows that of the ancient Greek translator.

stricken with illness and injury. By the time of Ben Sira's eulogy of the physician's craft, the influence of Greek medicine was beginning to be felt among Jews and the medical profession had become an independent, and largely 'secular', one. Medicine, and the arts of healing, had developed into a specialised skill, with an accompanying body of knowledge, that marked out the physician and pharmacist as 'wise' persons who possessed a corpus of learning appropriate to their work.

Earlier, however, this had not been the case in the ancient world generally, neither was it so in regard to the problems of disease and healing in Israel. Here it is abundantly clear that experience of sickness was closely bound up with ideas of divine displeasure and anger, and rather more directly, with a range of concepts concerning pollution, uncleanness and infringements of what pertained to 'the holy'.[2] Accordingly it appeared to be self-evident that those who were struck down by illness had in some way aroused God's anger, or had become affected by places or persons which were 'unclean'. It also appears to have been a very widely held assumption that certain persons, often unknown, were able to spread harmful influences of curse and destruction. The recognition that there could be immediate and local causes of harmful infections, therefore, in no way lessened the Israelite's basic conviction that disease emanated from God. The search for healing from such disease was then necessarily a search for the restoration of a secure and unhindered relationship with God.

In the larger world in which Israel grew up as a nation the concern with the often mysterious aspects of illness and disease greatly pre-occupied the ministers and priests of the cultus. This concerned both the identification of its causes and the proferring of appropriate methods of treatment. In both ancient Egypt and Mesopotamia special classes of priest were

---

2. For the understanding of health, healing and medicine in the Old Testament a number of useful studies are available. Cf. especially D. J. Wiseman, 'Medicine in the Old Testament', *Medicine and the Bible*, ed. B. Palmer, (Exeter: Paternoster Press, 1986), pp. 13–42. Very important in this regard are the anthropological studies of Mary Douglas, *Purity and Danger*; H. C. Kee, *Medicine, Miracle and Magic in New Testament Times*, (Cambridge: Cambridge University Press, 1986), especially pp. 9–26.

available to provide instruction and aid for those who had been struck down by illness.[3]

Their healing skills were of many kinds, some of them representing considerable knowledge of pharmacology, whereas other activities bordered on the magical. These latter included a resort to incantations and spells which could counter the source of the infection and help to drive out the evil spirit which had occasioned it. Along with such largely verbal expertise, however, these priestly ministrants sometimes appear to have possessed considerable manipulative skills in treating certain types of injury and infection. Undoubtedly there grew up a significant store of knowledge concerning the properties of healing herbs, the value of cleansing wounds, and of avoiding the spread of infectious conditions, coupled with the need for avoiding unfamiliar and poisonous foods.

We also find that such primitive religious practitioners of the healing arts clearly recognised the importance of restoring the morale of the unfortunate victim and of using various narcotic preparations in order to soften pain and to assist natural healing processes. It is also worthy of consideration that people were clearly aware that the roots of some sicknesses lay in disorders of the mind, as the stories involving Saul's periodic bouts of 'madness' illustrate (1 Sam. 16:14–23; 18:10f).[4]

Overall we can assume that men and women in antiquity fell victim to disease as frequently as they have done throughout human history and were both frightened and often mystified by the suddenness with which it could strike. It is wholly to be expected therefore that any concern with a wise and beneficent order of the world should have concerned itself with trying to understand how disease could be avoided, and how, when it struck, it could be overcome and the sufferer could be healed.

We can go further than this, however, since, if wisdom was concerned to understanding the fundamental order of the world, this imposed a uniquely strong intellectual demand to

3. For the Babylonian situation it is instructive that the celebrated law code of Hammurabi included a section of punishments for surgical malpractice; cf. *The Babylonian Laws*, ed. G. R. Driver and J. C. Miles, Vol. I, 416–420; Vol. II, pp. 79–81.

4. J. V. Kinnier Wilson, 'Medicine in the Land and Times of the Old Testament', *Studies in the Period of David and Solomon and Other Essays*, ed. T. Ishida (Winona Lake: Eisenbrauns, 1982), p. 359 has suggested with

understand those experiences and forces which appeared to disrupt and threaten the beneficent shape of such order. It was a fundamental conviction of the teachers of wisdom that the created order of the world was good and was conducive to a long and happy life for those men and women who shaped their lives according to its dictates.

In pursuing such knowledge it is evident that any claim to possess an understanding of the world's order would find it essential to be clear what links and connections there were between sin and disease. Both were regarded as affected by the relationship to God. It was important therefore that distinctions should be noted between uncleanness in its more formal cultic application which could be defined, and sudden bouts of infection which were life-threatening in their effect. All of this merely highlights the fact that a very complex world of concepts and associations existed concerning ideas of purity and danger.

God the Healer

When we turn to the pages of the Hebrew Bible we find that sickness and disease are in no way sharply distinguished from sin and wrongdoing. This is made strikingly evident to the reader of modern English versions in connection with the very significant passage of Isa. 53:3-5. The familiar words in the description of the servant of the Lord as one who was 'a man of sorrows and acquainted with grief' (Isa. 53:3 RSV) have become in the NRSV 'a man of suffering and acquainted with infirmity'. The response made by those who benefit from the servant's misfortune is then expressed in the words:

> 'Surely he has borne our infirmities
> and carried our diseases.'
> Isa. 53:4 (NRSV)

This is then extended yet further in the following verse to make it clear that the servant's sufferings have borne away not only

---

reference to Ps. 56 that the psalm speaker may have been suffering from some mental illness.

the griefs and diseases of his people, but also their transgressions (v. 6).

Overall the important feature is not that 'sickness' should be emphasised more than 'grief' or 'transgression' in describing the servant's achievements. Rather all three are viewed as part of a single inextricably intertwined chain of misfortune where every one of these aspects is intended to be referred to. Disease, sin, and the pain consequent upon misfortune generally, are regarded as different aspects of one interconnected whole. This whole is the realm of death and sin which sums up the range of experiences which threaten human beings and separates them from the life-giving, healing and forgiving power of God.[5]

It is against a background of such thought that we can properly understand the very positive assertions of the Old Testament that it is the Lord God who is the true Healer.[6] This is illustrated very fully in the short narrative of Exod. 15:22–26 which tells how Moses 'healed' the bitter waters of the desert spring Marah by putting into it the leaves of a tree which God had indicated to him. This made 'sweet' (v. 25) the water of the spring which had previously been undrinkable. We could easily find a modern rationalising explanation in arguing that Moses had put into the water the leaves of a plant which neutralised, or perhaps only disguised, the bitter taste which the spring waters had previously had.

The following verse, however, carries the significance of this action a very great deal further than this. The 'healing' of the waters of the spring has a become a pointer to the truth that God is the Healer, and this is so because diseases also derive from him:

'If you will diligently listen to the voice of the Lord your God, and do what he approves, giving attention to his commands and

---

5. For the concepts of life and death in the Old Testament cf. now especially M. A. Knibb, 'Life and Death in the Old Testament, *The World of Ancient Israel* (Cambridge: CUP, 1989), pp. 395–415; see also A. R. Johnson, *The Vitality of the Individual in the Thought of Ancient Israel* (2nd ed. Cardiff: Univ. of Wales Press, 1964), especially p. 87ff.

6. For the understanding of healing in the Old Testament, see now Brown, *TWAT*, VII, 617–625; H. J. Stoebe, *THAT*, II, 803–809; G. F. Hasel, 'Health and Healing in the Old Testament', *AUSSt* 21 (1983), pp. 191–202.

keeping all his laws, I will put none of the diseases upon you which I put upon the Egyptians; for I am the Lord, your Healer.'

Exod. 15:25–26

Clearly the divine title, God your Healer (*El-Ropheka*), is an ancient one associated with the location where the incident took place and the spring was situated, but there is a full implication that safe drinking water is a gift from God. As healing comes from God so also may disease arise from the same source.

There is a yet further striking illustration of this belief that it is the divine power which dispenses disease and destruction as well as healing and life in the prophetic description of God's appearance in a theophany:

His splendour was like the light,
   rays flashed from his hand;
   although his power was hidden.
Disease went before him,
   and plague followed behind.

Habb. 3:4–5

No doubt all of this was a necessary outworking of the strong Israelite belief in the divine sovereignty which felt impelled to ascribe all natural phenomena and experiences to an order of life which was wholly under divine control. There is therefore in the Old Testament a very firm awareness that both disease and healing come from the same source in God's own personal being.

A further indication of this is to be seen in the story of a life-threatening illness which befell king Hezekiah (2 Kgs. 20:1–11 = Isa. 38:1–22). The king is reported to have been stricken with a severe illness, apparently in the form of a boil, which first of all drew forth from the prophet Isaiah a very negative prognosis. However the king turned to God in complete submissiveness and pious trust and was then assured of a recovery and a renewed expectation of life. The healing process was aided by a modest application of medical treatment (2 Kgs. 20:7 = Isa. 38:21). Nevertheless throughout the story the primary assumption is that healing is a direct gift from God which had been made possible by the king's pious action.

Healing and piety are seen to go together in much the same way as do sickness and sin.

One of the most striking indications of the strength of feeling with which the belief that God was the only proper source of healing was adhered to is shown by the brief report concerning king Asa given by the Chronicler:

> In the thirty-ninth year of his reign Asa became diseased in his feet, and his disease was severe; yet even in his disease he did not seek the Lord, but sought help from the physicians.
>
> 2 Chron. 16:12

This report is one of the relatively few to indicate that there existed in Israel a class of physicians which was separate from the cultus. It furthermore demonstrates that to resort to such persons for help was looked upon as a betrayal of loyalty to the Lord God of Israel, and so was viewed as a form of apostasy. The belief that the God of Israel alone was the appropriate source of healing for one who worshipped him is taken with the utmost seriousness.

A rather different story, which nevertheless makes the same assumption, is told of Elisha in 2 Kgs. 5:1–19 concerning Naaman, a Syrian military commander who was healed from a dangerous, and disfiguring, skin disease. The Lord, the God of Israel, is the true Healer.[7] It is against such a background that we can best grasp the proper import of the strong interest shown by the wisdom tradition in the art of healing.

Healing and the Cultus

In order to grasp the complex world of thought which underlies the Old Testament's attitude to disease and healing it is necessary to recognise that there existed a firmly rooted sense of continuity and wholeness which pervaded all life. Penetrating through this overall continuum of concepts and ideas was a deep-seated dualism. On one side was ranged the realm of life, which comprehended not only the vitality of all creatures and

---

7. For the significance of this in exhibiting the relationships between religion, magic and healing cf. A. Rofé, *The Prophetical Stories* (Jerusalem: Magnes Press, 1988), 128f.

plants, and which distinguished these from inanimate objects, but it included those features which served to promote and protect life. Accordingly it included concepts of blessing, wholeness, fertility, general wellbeing (Heb. *shalom*) and health. All such desirable conditions of existence enabled human beings to achieve the goal of 'a long life' (Heb. *'erekh yamim*, literally 'length of days').

Set over against this was the realm of death. As we might expect for a realm that opposed life, this included not only the final event of death itself, but also those many aspects of experience which were life-threatening. Accordingly it included disease, uncleanness, barrenness and other forms of bodily impairment such as blindness and lameness. It was a realm of 'curse', just as the realm of life was one of 'blessing'.

This is not to argue that there was no clear distinction made between these basic concepts, since their relative distinctness is abundantly evident. Rather the main point is that there was a degree of continuity between them which entailed that ideas concerning them often overlapped. Certainly too a closely similar attitude was shown regarding each of them, demanding that they be countered by resort to the life-renewing power of God. Health and healing were aspects of 'life' and all that threatened and opposed this were aspects of death.[8]

It is within this world of ideas that we can best understand the importance of cultus.[9] Central to this was the conviction that the Lord the God of Israel, was 'the Living God', which meant that he was a source of life and that his gifts were such as to promote and protect life.[10] That which pertained to 'death' was hostile to this and threatened the holiness and effectiveness

---

8. For the broad biblical understanding of death, together with its mythological associations, cf. Lloyd R. Bailey, Sr., *Biblical Perspectives on Death*, Overtures to Biblical Theology, (Philadelphia: Fortress Press, 1979), pp. 23ff. N. Tromp, *Primitive Conceptions of Death and the Netherworld in the Old Testament* (Rome: Pontifical Institute Press, 1969).

9. An excellent treatment of the intellectual assumptions that undergirded Israelite cultus is to be found in F. H. Gorman, Jr., *The Ideology of Ritual*, JSOTSupp 91 (Sheffield: JSOT Press, 1990). Cf. also K. Seybold, *Introducing the Psalms*, ET R. G. Dunphy (Edinburgh: T. & T. Clark, 1990), pp. 177ff.

10. The significance of this terminology is studied very extensively in S. Kreuzer, *Der lebendige Gott*, BWANT VI, 16 (116) (Stuttgart—Berlin: W. Kohlhammer, 1983).

of all cultic activity. Not surprisingly therefore the onset of death and the necessary funeral rites which marked the passage of a human being to the world of 'the ancestors' (Lit. 'fathers') was a very sensitive time.

Similarly the experience of new life which occurred with the birth of a child was a very significant moment, not only of joyfulness, but also of danger since the mysterious interface between life and death was being crossed. No doubt all of this was strongly assisted by the awareness that childbearing and childbirth was a difficult, and often dangerous, experience (cf. Gen. 3:16).

The major transition stages of life: birth, puberty, marriage and death were all subject to important ritual activities. So also, however, were the more haphazard and unforeseen experiences of life such as occurred with illness or major injuries. The Old Testament abundantly testifies to the fact that such experiences were usually occasions for visits to the sanctuary and for the offering of special prayers for recovery and divine help.[11] All of this has been richly noted in connection with studies of the Old Testament Psalter, where it may be regarded as certain that a considerable number of psalms of lament, set out as prayers of individual persons, were primarily intended to be used in time of such misfortune.

One of the most striking instances of such prayers from a person struck down by illness is to be found in Psalms 38:

> There is no health in my body because of your anger;
>   there is no life in my body because of my sin.
> My wrongful deeds reach over my head;
>   They weigh like a burden too heavy for me.
> My wounds grow foul and fester because of my folly,
>   I am utterly bowed down and knocked out;
>   all the day I go about mourning.
> For my body is filled with burning,
>   and there is no health in my being.

---

11. K. Seybold and U. B. Mueller, *Sickness and Healing*, Biblical Encounters Series, ET D. W. Stott (Nashville: Abingdon Press, 1981). For Ps. 38 cf. especially pp. 44f. See now also K. Seybold, *Introducing the Psalms*, pp. 82ff. Seybold's fullest discussion of the subject is to be found in *Das Gebet des Kranken im Alten Testament*, BWANT 99 (Stuttgart: W. Kohlhammer, 1973).

I am utterly worn out and crushed;
I groan because of the torment in my mind (lit. 'heart').

Psalm 38:3–8

There could hardly be a clearer expression of the close inter-connection that was felt to exist between sin and sickness. Yet the stricken worshipper was encouraged to present his pleas to God, not simply to find comfort in doing so, but because it was from God that healing was expected to come. Overall the range of direct medical knowledge and treatment that was available for the sick in ancient Israel appears to have been surprisingly limited, in spite of the reference to a form of treatment in Isa. 38:21. More particularly there was evidently a strong discour-agement against looking outside the priestly ministry of the cultus in order to secure other kinds of medical attention, whether or not they involved questionable practices of a semi-magical nature.

It is also of considerable importance for an understanding of the manner in which the teachers of wisdom have handled and developed concepts of life and healing to recognise that many psalms include special pleas for deliverance from death and Sheol (the realm of the departed).[12] It has become increasingly evident that these urgent requests were often, and perhaps usually, prayers for recovery from illness, rather than requests to be granted a safe passage to a realm of the blessed dead in another world. They mark part of the continuing, and deeply felt, conflict between forces of life and death which faced every human being in daily life. Death was not simply the end-point of a human life, to be viewed as a distant inevitability, but rather an ever-present force which threatened all human existence in this world.

The close connection between cultic activity and this life-death struggle made resort to God in prayer a primary means of seeking medical assistance and in many cases the only one that was available for the ancient Israelite. Recognising this fact provides a helpful background for a better understanding of

---

12. Cf. C. F. Barth, *Introduction to the Psalms*, ET R. A. Wilson (Oxford: B. H. Blackwell, 1966, pp. 49ff. Barth's fuller treatment of the subject is to be found in *Die Errettung von Tode in die individuellen Klage—und Dankliedern des Alten Testament* (Zollikon: Evangelischer Verlag, 1947).

the distinctiveness of what wisdom had to teach about health and healing. We have accepted that the early wisdom of Israel had no particular anti-cultic bias, although it represented a stream of intellectual life that was not primarily concerned with cultic concepts and ideas. It simply inherited a world of ideas and expectations which took the role of the cultus for granted. However, as we have already noted in connection with the strong concern shown by the teachers of wisdom to grasp the essential nature of things and to observe their inter-relationships, the wise also strove to obtain a comprehensive world-view which was compatible with their own particular aims and intentions.

It is in the light of this concern that we can see that the possibility existed among the wise for a very different understanding of the nature of sickness and disease from that nurtured by the priesthood, and more directly for a separation of the concept of sickness from that of sin.

In two particular areas we could reasonably presume that the pursuit of wisdom lent to it a particular interest in health and healing. The first of these was the fact that certain areas of the pursuit of knowledge were concerned with classes of natural phenomena, especially in plant and animal life (cf. 1 Kgs. 4:33). Inevitably such knowledge impinged on areas of concern to the pharmacist, with the desire to recognize the healing properties of certain plants, or even their narcotic effect.[13] A deep-seated belief that unique patterns of correspondence pertained throughout much of the natural world encouraged the widespread conviction that there existed natural herbal remedies and antidotes to many, if not all, types of illness. Clearly this was of direct interest to the teachers of wisdom who demonstrated a very sharply observant attitude to all aspects of natural life.

However, even more directly impinging on areas of interest to the wise, was the concern with the efficacy of words and signs as imbued with forms of 'magical' power. In general it is

---

13. The question of the use of narcotic drugs in the world of the ancient Near East, including Israel, can easily be greatly exaggerated. I regard this to be generally true of the suggestions proposed by M. Field, *Angels and Ministers of Grace* (London: Longmans, 1971). Nevertheless the knowledge and use of

not entirely practicable to make sharp distinctions between ideas of magic and religion in antiquity, since there was clearly no widely recognised dividing line between the two. Rather the two areas represent trends, and even attitudes of expectation, rather than firmly marked out and distinct realms.[14] Prayers could be regarded as little more than incantations and rituals could easily be treated as necessarily effective means of warding off danger. Even objects could be treated as though they were filled with a special potency when in the hands of the right person (cf. Elisha's staff; 2 Kgs. 4:29, 31).

In spite of the difficulty in making a clear demarcation between magic and religion in the popular faith of ancient Israel, it is important that we should recognise that the main trend of the teaching of wisdom was towards the discouraging of magical expectations. Overall therefore the pursuit of wisdom was a constructive factor in challenging and repudiating popular magical practices and belief. The deep-seated concern of the wise to recognise a coherent and cohesive order pervading all things, and especially to urge the primary importance of responsible moral behaviour throughout all areas of experience, left little room for a magical approach to the needs and alarms of daily life.

It must be recognised that, of all the aspects of human experience which tended to promote and preserve the belief in magical, and semi-magical, practices, those involving illness had the greatest popularity. The suddenness with which sickness could strike, the feeling of helplessness which the victim suffered, and not least the confused and disoriented state of mind to which he, or she, was brought by it, promoted interest in the search for magical cures. As so many forms of human society have demonstrated, the healing arts have frequently been closely linked to those of witchcraft and sorcery!

That such was the case in ancient Israel, at least in a particular stratum of society is strongly suggested by the Israelite women whom the prophet Ezekiel condemns in Ezek. 13:13–23. It is noteworthy that they are said to prophesy 'in the

such drugs, especially as aids to healing, was clearly widespread in the ancient world.
14. Cf. M. Douglas, *Purity and Danger*, pp. 58ff.

hunt for souls'. However their activities included the sewing of magic bands upon the wrists of people and covering their victims' heads with veils. What exactly the purpose of all this was is not made clear by the prophet's rebuke, but it is very likely that these were attempts to induce healing by semi-magical means.[15] All the more is this probable, since a primary deprivation for those taken in exile to Babylon was their separation from the more formal features of worship in the Jerusalem temple. Falling ill became a serious problem.

The relationship between wisdom and magic is one that suggests that, as with prophecy and the cultus, the dividing lines were often hard to draw. Nevertheless it is highly probable that, not only was the pursuit of a true and effective wisdom a strong disincentive to magic and the expectations which its practices aroused in ancient Israel, but also that concern with sickness and healing was one of the foremost areas where this disincentive operated.

Wisdom as the Path of Life

There is already in the early proverbial teaching a quite striking affirmation of the teaching of wisdom as something that promoted 'life', whereas to ignore, or oppose, it represented choosing the path of 'death'. Already therefore the groundwork existed for a significant take-over of basic ideas which had wide currency in cultic activities and for linking them directly to the teaching of the wise:

> In the path of right action is life,
> but the way of folly leads to death.
> Prov. 12:28

> The instruction of the wise is a fountain of life,
> that one may avoid the snares of death.
> Prov. 13:14; cf. also 14:27

What we have here is the relatively familiar dualism between life and death which marked the whole world-view of the

---

15. Ezek.13:17–23. Cf. W. Zimmerli, *Ezekiel 1*, Hermeneia (Philadelphia: Fortress Press, 1979), pp. 296f.

ancient Israelite. Clearly God was on the side of 'life', but so too was the teaching of wisdom. To a significant degree also it is arguable that, as the promotion of instruction in the dictates of wisdom progressed, so too would it make apparent the fact that the assumptions of wisdom differed considerably on this matter from those of the cultus. The quasi-physical nature of the life and health-giving properties of the cultus are very clearly shown in the great outpouring of 'the river of life' which the prophet Ezekiel envisioned as flowing out from under the entrance of the temple. In symbolic language it portrays the manner in which the 'life' of the cultus was capable of being understood in terms of welfare, fertility and healing:

> And wherever the river flows every living creature which abounds will live, and there will be an abundance of fish; for this water flows there, that the water of the sea may become fresh; so everything will live where the river flows.
>
> . . .
>
> And on the banks, on both sides of the river, there will grow all kinds of trees for food. Their leaves will not wither nor their fruit fail, but they will bear fresh fruit every month, because the water from the sanctuary flows for them. Their fruit will be for food, and their leaves for healing.
>
> Ezek. 47:9,12

What is striking in this highly symbolised vision of the benefits that the worship of the restored Jerusalem temple is to bring is the manner in which it illustrates the connections between life, the productivity of the soil and healing.[16]

We obtain a further very similar picture of the traditional belief that worship and obedience to God ensured a general condition of wellbeing from what is promised as the result of the Lord God's blessing in Deut. 28:1–14. Contrastingly those who disobey God and incur his anger are threatened with the consequences of curse (Deut. 28:15–68). Significant among such consequences is the occurrence of disease:

---

16. Cf. W. Zimmerli, *Ezekiel 2*, Hermeneia (Philadelphia: Fortress Press, 1983), pp. 513f. Zimmerli detects a considerable degree of expansion of the prophet's original vision in this section.

The Lord will make disease cling to you until he has destroyed you from off the land which you are about to enter and of which you will take possession.

Deut. 28:21; cf. also vv. 22-24

It is in the light of these broadly based assertions that obedience to God and worship at his sanctuary constitute the proper ways to secure life and good health that we can best understand the distinctiveness of the earlier wisdom teaching concerning life and health. Certainly we find that the claim that to follow the dictates of wisdom is the way to secure life is prominently presented:

The fruit of right-dealing persons is a tree of life.
but wrongdoing takes away lives.

Prov. 11:30

We should not be misled into thinking that the familiar mythological image concerning a 'tree of life' has been reduced to the level of a metaphor and left with only vague meaning. There would appear to be a strong intention of insisting that right actions tend towards healthy living and so can help to promote a long life.

This is even more fully brought out in a number of direct references to the assurance that the teaching of the wise serves as medicine and promotes health:

A calm disposition gives life to the body,
but bad feelings make the body ill.[17]

Prov. 14:30

This already points us in the direction of the particular interest shown by the wise in the disciplining of the mind to maintain a calm and controlled disposition:

---

17. W. McKane, *Proverbs*, pp. 232, 272 translates: 'A tranquil mind promotes good health, but jealousy (promotes) decay in the bones'. However I have taken the noun '*qinah*–jealousy' to have a wider significance than our conventional 'jealousy' and to indicate many types of bad (and strong) emotion.

A cheerful mind is good medicine,
   but a depressed spirit withers the body.[18]
                          Prov. 17:22

In a similar fashion the right use of speech to establish a
happy and contented frame of mind is tantamount to healing
(Prov. 12:18; cf. also Prov. 16:24). It is recognised that positive
and happy relationships are conducive to good health. Over
against this, deep disappointment or personal humiliation
(Heb. describes such as 'a broken spirit') can be far worse than
the experience of sickness:

A man's spirit will endure illness;
   but a broken spirit who can bear?
                          Prov. 18:14

The idea here may simply be that physical forms of illness
are temporary but deep emotional hurt may be much more
lasting and injurious in its effects. Even so the implication is
clearly that the inner hurt of a broken spirit is worse than
physical sickness and may be far more difficult to heal. The
familiar anxiety of the teachers of wisdom to urge proper care
in speech and a right empathy for others is defended as part of a
larger concern for good health.
   Overall the older teaching of wisdom shared much of the
dualistic tendency which the cult had encouraged regarding the
necessity for promoting 'life' in all its manifestations and
avoiding the actions and attitudes which led to 'death'. Among
these actions and attitudes were those which were recognised as
hurtful of relationships or indifferent to the proper care of the
body. The pursuit of wisdom was believed to follow a path
which led to long life and happiness.

The Significance of Sickness and Healing in Post-exilic Wisdom

We have already noted that the link between illness and the
cultus was so strong in early Israel that resort to physicians

---

18. McKane's translation (*ibid.*, pp. 238, 506) is striking: 'Inner happiness
makes for good health, but jealousy promotes decay in the bones.'

outside the monopoly on its treatment claimed by the priesthood was viewed as serious disloyalty towards God. If God were alone the true healer, than it was necessary to seek his help in time of sickness through his appointed ministers. Yet the great political and social upheaval that came to Israel with the destruction of the Jerusalem temple in 587 BCE led to an ever-increasing spread of large numbers of Jews living outside the range of its cultic ministry. What then were men and women to do when they fell ill? Clearly deprivation from the cultus and its benefits could be a serious problem.

Already we have noted the conventional categorisation of a foreign land, unblest by the approved places and forms of divine worship, as one that was 'unclean'. Our argument has been that this placed a very significant number of former Judean citizens in a situation which we can only describe as that of liminality. They had been taken from a safe and secure world that was rendered holy by proper worship. Instead they had been set down in an environment where places, persons and activities were rendered 'unclean'. This uncleanness was especially viewed as imposing a severe risk of illness. It was made all the more acute by the close proximity of non-Jewish neighbours, the situation in which many Jews now found themselves. These neighbours would have pursued patterns of worship which were tainted with paganism. How were Jews to cope with such a threat?

One way was undoubtedly through the gradual development and organisation of patterns of worship, overseen by former priests, which could provide a temporary compensation for what had been lost. This seems to be what is implied by Ezekiel's assurance that God had become 'a sanctuary for a little while' (or 'a little sanctuary') to those who had been taken to Babylon (Ezek. 11:16). Overall, however, it is clear that such a changed circumstance imposed immense stresses upon the inherited thought world of Jews, which had been shaped by the cultus and its services. Surely nowhere was the acuteness of this situation more likely to have been sharply felt than in the case of illness!

It is against such a background that we can interpret the quite unique emphasis of the broad affirmations concerning the strategy and benefits of wisdom in Prov. 1–9. Wisdom provides a pattern for living which makes possible a long and healthy life:

> My son, do not forget my teaching,
>   let your heart keep my commandments;
> for length of days and years of life
>   and abundant wellbeing they will give you.
> Let not integrity and steadfastness forsake you;
>   tie them around your neck,
>   write them on the tablet of your heart.
>   Prov. 3:1–3

> It will be health to your flesh
>   and vitality to your body.
>   Prov. 3:8

> Long life is in her right hand;
>   in her left hand are riches and honour.
>   Prov. 3:16

> She (wisdom) is a tree of life to those who lay hold of her;
>   those who hold her fast are called happy.
>   Prov. 3:18

> My son, be attentive to my words;
>   incline your ear to my sayings.
> Let them not slip from your sight;
>   keep them in your mind.
> For they are life to him who finds them,
>   and healing to all his flesh.
>   Prov. 4:20–22

> The fear of the Lord is the beginning of wisdom,
>   and the knowledge of the Holy One is insight.
> For by me your days will be multiplied,
>   and years will be added to your life.
> If you are wise, it is yourself that benefits;
>   if you scoff, you alone will pay the price.
>   Prov. 9:10–12

Although the teaching here is of a broad and general character, and could presumably have been presented by the wise at almost any period in Israel's history, these introductory didactic poems on wisdom are almost certainly of post-exilic origin. Their special interest does not so much lie in the individual components of their teaching, but rather in the way in which they have sought to provide a comprehensive portrait of what wisdom is all about. In doing so, there has obviously been a major effort to combine together the basic concepts of piety, morality and practical good sense to form a charter for living.

A primary requirement therefore is that the reader should respect wisdom and those who teach it. For this to happen a yet more fundamental attitude of mind is required. This is to be found in 'the fear of the Lord' which is the 'starting point' (beginning) of wisdom (Prov. 1:7; 9:10). Only when this piety is present will the right mental attitude be available for the guidelines of wisdom to be nurtured. Only then will the good morals and the long life which wisdom proffers become possible. At the same time we have already noted how the original cultic features of this 'fear of the Lord' have undergone a basic shift of meaning. Although no intention appears to be present to set aside the belief that piety will naturally express itself in formal allegiance to the cultus, there has been a major change of emphasis and understanding.

This change of emphasis shows itself most fully in regard to ideas of life, health and healing. All these latter benefits are now part of a very much broader, and more personally demanding, life-style which the wise have outlined. In constructing such an intellectual system of ideas the teachers of wisdom have both simplified and integrated a very much wider and more complex range of concepts. That which is 'good' is that which promotes 'life', and this life which wisdom promises brings together various notions and beliefs concerning the avoidance of what is dangerous and harmful. To this extent the positive benefits of following the precepts of wisdom are continually in need of being defined by reference to their opposites. These comprise all that leads to death and ruination.

So wisdom has begun a process of systematising ideas on the themes of virtue and wellbeing which had not previously formed part of any system. On the contrary, ideas of uncleanness, abomination, evil, violence and disease had all belonged to a very confused and ill-defined world of what threatened danger and harm to the unprincipled or unwary. In sum, wisdom showed the path which avoided the way to 'death'. It was therefore itself the right path to a long life, happiness and general wellbeing.

The very fact that such notions subsume and greatly modify earlier notions which were directly related to cultic activity fully bears out our main contention that wisdom had begun a process of 'de-sanctifying' and 'de-mystifying' a number of basic areas of human understanding. These had previously largely been the province of the priesthood and cultus. In the urgent necessity to cater for the daily life of Jews which could no longer rely on immediate and direct access to the sanctuary of the temple and the ministry of its priests a process of 'secularising' and isolating from cultic activity had been set in train.

Job, the Righteous Sufferer

The book of Job is a work of many-sided artistry and the extent to which it can be studied as a characteristic product of wisdom, or interpreted as primarily focused upon problems with which the wise sought to deal, have all been questioned. It is certainly a work of post-exilic origin, although it may well contain in its rich poetry themes and traditions from a much earlier date. So also its concern with the pains and turmoil of the human situation, and its desire to present a measure of theodicy for human suffering, have shown themselves to be concerns which are in evidence throughout a long period of the ancient Near East. It is a work which explores many aspects of the human scene, both in its practical and intellectual features. In general it has been interpreted as a poetic disquisition upon the theme of human suffering.[19]

In pursuing this goal it appears to make use of an old tradition about a righteous sufferer and it uses the speeches of Job's friends in order to explore the possibilities of finding an explanation for the painful side of human existence. It must be regarded as a work of such a distinctive kind that it is far from easy to incorporate what it has to say on its chosen subject into the tradition of Israelite wisdom more generally. However,

---

19. There is an immense range of studies on the Book of Job. Among the most recent Edwin M. Good, *In Turns of Tempest. A Reading of Job* (Stanford: Stanford University Press, 1990), may be especially mentioned.

from the perspective of an interest in what the teachers of wisdom had to say about health and healing it is a work of some significance. This arises primarily from the fact that, although it describes the nature of Job's misfortunes and misery as brought on from many sides and several eventualities, it focuses the critical nature of his plight in terms of affliction with severe sickness. So Job has the misfortune to find that his large estate is ruined by foreign marauders (Job 1:15) and his servants killed (Job 1:17). His house has been destroyed in a storm and his children lie dead within it (Job 1:19). Such dire disasters could hardly become more acute. Yet in fact these catastrophes are apparently not the worst of Job's afflictions. Significantly his plight is regarded as made even more acute by his being personally stricken with a very painful disease:

> Then satan answered the Lord, 'skin for skin! All that a person has he will give for his life. So put forth your hand now, and touch his bone and his flesh, and he will curse you to your face.' Then the Lord said to satan, 'Behold he is in your power; only spare his life.'
> Job 2:4–6

So Job is struck down by loathsome sores all over his body (Job 2:7) and he experiences all the misery and alienation which his condition imposes on him. Some of the most poignant of Job's bitter cries are those which describe the physical misery and humiliation which his condition has brought on (Job 19:1–22). The speeches of his friends also give an alarming picture of the wretchedness, and sense of helplessness, which such sickness entails.

Throughout the poems there is never any suggestion that there could be any other being responsible for what has happened to Job than God himself. At the same time there is no clear indication that any very useful medical help was available, or that, during his suffering, any immediate prospect of the recovery which eventually took place was entertained. Job is severely ill; his condition has been brought on, if not directly by God at least with divine sufferance, and there is no evident hope of any alleviation for the distress. Job's condition, in fact,

---

Good particularly warns against assuming too readily that Job is to be understood as essentially a product of the Israelite wisdom tradition.

is presented as one that must have been fairly typical of many such persons in ancient Israel.

The assumption that God must in a real sense be the effective cause of Job's distress, if only because he has allowed it to happen, lends force to the poem and enables the discussion of the problem between Job and his friends to assume the form of a theodicy.[20] Job's complaint is consistently that he has committed no offence against God which could have occasioned his misfortune. The argument of his friends is that he must have done, even if he had done so in an unwitting and unrecognised manner.

From the perspective of a concern with wisdom and healing there is a special interest in that Job's experience of sickness is highlighted as one that is most personally felt, and therefore the most terrifying, because most life-threatening, of all his misfortunes. Job is not simply a righteous sufferer. He is one who suffers acutely with some extremely painful disease which incapacitates and humiliates him. It forces him to withdraw completely from all normal life, whether of a business or social kind. Illness is alienation from human society and, seemingly, from God!

Clearly those interpreters of the book who have recognised in it a profound concern with all aspects of human suffering, and with the problem of the divine governance of the world, have not been mistaken. The author of the book of Job paints his picture with large and sweeping brush-strokes. Yet it is well worthy of consideration that the issues with which he deals, and the answers that he endeavours to apprehend, are not simply of this broad and universal character. It is in a real sense a book about sickness, if only because it singles out this type of human misfortune as one that is especially personal and acute.

Most scholars have recognised that the author cannot be said to have succeeded, if his intention was to find an explanation for human suffering and misfortune generally. The problems are too widespread and the limits of human probing of the mind of the Creator are such that it is not possible to draw clear and firm conclusions. If the discussion between satan and God

---

20. It is important also for a proper understanding of the prayer of Hezekiah in Isa. 38:9–20 that the writer takes for granted the belief that God is in a

as to the genuinely disinterested nature of Job's piety offers some clue (Job 2:3), it is only a modestly satisfying one. That faith in the face of adversity provides a very strong argument for disinterested piety is clearly beyond question. However, there is reason to suspect that the author's purpose lay not in reaching deep and ultimate conclusions about all human suffering, but rather in establishing the parameters within which certain aspects of it should be understood.

In this regard it is of significance that the most acute manifestation of Job's suffering is described in the form of disease. The reason why this should be the case must surely lie in the perception that, whereas some forms of human misery can be regarded as in the nature of self-inflicted wounds, illness and disease usually cannot be so explained.

All the more was this the case in antiquity where, in spite of obvious efforts to avoid harmful foods and unhealthy patterns of living, the causes of disease remained an almost complete mystery. This must have become increasingly the case once serious efforts were made by the wisdom teachers to identify and classify various forms and kinds of evil. If the general contention is correct, which has been accepted here in the wake of views presented by many scholars, that Israelite wisdom pursued a strongly moralistic path, then the problem of 'non-moral' misfortune became acute.

If bad actions produced bad results, as the teachers of wisdom were certain they did, then what was to be said about bad results which could not be said to have been occasioned by bad actions? If an answer to such questions were not reasonably accessible, then at least it would help to be able to identify the kinds of misfortune which did not have a morally negative cause. To identify sickness, at least in some of its forms, as such a misfortune which lacked a moral explanation was an important intellectual advance. It does not remove sickness and disease from the areas of life controlled by divine sovereignty, but it separates them from the mysterious spheres of guilt and wrongdoing.

For earlier generations of Israelites the dangers of 'unclean-

---

fundamental sense the author of the sickness which the king has experienced. Accordingly, piety is reckoned as an important feature of the path to healing.

ness', or of failing to observe the rules of 'abomination' when eating cooked sacrificial meat,[21] may have helped provide some understanding of the sources of sickness. Similarly the way in which infection could be contagious, or could easily spread from one object to another, were observable. All of these precautions had been part of the levitical tradition of 'medical' lore. The danger of infecting open wounds and the need for cleansing them were also not too difficult to identify. Yet in spite of all such precautions. the causes of most forms of illness remained cloaked in mystery. Many forms of disease struck suddenly and with no apparent cause. As the teachers of wisdom had sought strenuously to moralise the older notions of taboo and 'abomination' which the cult had fostered, so now they sought to advance a stage further. Sickness and disease were to be separated out from other kinds of misfortune for which there was a clearly recognisable moral cause.

Is it then not a particular feature of the book of Job that it especially singles out physical sickness as a kind of human suffering which cannot be directly related to sin? Two main features of the wisdom tradition have forced the author to recognise this point. The first of these is the progressive way in which ideas of sin and wrongdoing have been given a truly moral quality. The idea of 'unwitting' and 'inadvertant' sin has fallen by the wayside. For the teachers of wisdom wrongdoing is a moral matter and so sin is not be taken seriously if it is a purely accidental error. Its roots lie in human intentions, a point which the authors of proverbial wisdom were at pains to stress.

The second point is of comparable importance: for the post-exilic wisdom tradition the ideas of sickness and disease have become progressively detached from the cultus and its concerns. That sickness and health are matters of wide human and public concern was increasingly evident. They were no longer issues that could be left in the hands of an official priesthood and which could be treated as part of a monopoly of levitical knowledge. It is no surprise therefore that we find Job

---

21. Cf. Ezek. 4:9–17, which offers an instructive example of the close correlation between holiness and cleanness in respect of food.

on the rubbish heap at the edge of town, rather than in the sanctuary appealing, like the speaker of Ps. 38, for forgiveness from God! The subject of sickness and disease has, like Job himself, come out into the open!

Seen in such a light, it is noteworthy that Job's problem is one that especially concerns sickness and disease, and that it becomes less clear-cut and answerable once it is treated as part of the more abstract problem of human suffering generally. It must be admitted that this latter, broader, issue cannot be ignored, but it is arguable that the author of the Job poem has achieved something of importance towards gaining a better understanding of wisdom and health.

The author of Prov. 9:10–12 had been excessively confident that the questions of good health and a long life could be answered quite personally and directly in terms of following, or rejecting, the precepts of wisdom. To some extent this could be seen to be true. Fools walked in slippery places and suffered as a result! Yet, in looking for a comprehensive set of guidelines for a long and healthy life, the teachers of wisdom, had been guilty of brash over-confidence when it came to dealing with matters of health and healing. It was clearly one of the most complex and seemingly intractable, of all human problems. Disease knew no moral rules in choosing where to strike. The belief that God must himself be, in some vague sense, the author of disease, simply added to the problem.

What the author of the book of Job has achieved is a firm case for separating the problems of physical illness and disease from the wider range of issues related to moral wrongdoing and cultic steadfastness. Job could be both an exemplary wise man, and one of unchallenged piety and devotion. Yet he could, nevertheless, be the victim of a most severe and disabling disease. This cast no discredit on him, but simply required a recognition that not all forms of human misfortune could be regarded as self-inflicted. While it achieves rather less than solving the unanswerable problem of why good persons may endure great suffering, it nevertheless makes a significant advance in human understanding. It does so by recognising that sickness and disease represent a very distinctive kind of evil which cannot be comprehended within the more easily recognisable moral norms.

The Critical Mind of Qoheleth

By the latter half of the third century BCE Jewish thought had
begun to be influenced by contact with Hellenistic ideas and
teaching. As one feature of this there arose a distinctive type of
popular teaching and argument, based on the traditions of
wisdom, but undoubtedly influenced also by the style and
attitudes of popular Hellenistic preachers.[22] At this level there
was not so much an effective integration of Jewish and
Hellenistic ideas, but rather a similarity of themes and
rhetorical styles.

It is within this new world of ideas and conventions that the
contribution of the third-century teacher Qoheleth can best be
understood. Our interest in what he has to say about wisdom
and health is almost entirely taken up with what he has to say
concerning death.[23] At first glance the subject appears to hold
his attention in almost too strong a fashion. He revels in
holding out to the reader, often assumed to be a young person
full of enthusiasm for life, a consciousness that he, or she, must
one day die (cf. Qoh. 3:16–22).

Some of this is undoubtedly to be regarded as a rhetorical
ploy, since a recognition of mortality forces a degree of
attention to the basic question about the purpose and goals of
living. However, there are certain features which are of special
interest to the question of what wisdom has to teach regarding
life and death and the connection of this with matters of health
and disease. The first of these is the fact, which at first may not
appear surprising, that Qoheleth treats of death in a wholly
unmythological fashion. Death for him is simply the end-point
of a life. It heralds a passage into another world where what lies
in store cannot be known (Qoh. 3:22). Only when we reflect
back upon the older, and heavily mythological, associations of
the concept of death in early Israel do we realise the extent of
his innovation. Death is no longer a daily threat, but is quite
openly regarded as an inevitable terminal point for each human

---

22. Cf. M. Hengel, *Judaism and Hellenism*, ET J. Bowden, (London: SCM
Press, 1974), Vol. 1, pp. 115ff.
23. Cf. J. L. Crenshaw, 'The Shadow of Death in Qoheleth', *Israelite
Wisdom. Essays in Honor of S. Terrien*, (Missoula: Scholars Press, 1978),
pp. 205–216.

life. It marks a closure—a necessary point for seeking a summing-up and assessment of what life has achieved.

For Qoheleth therefore death is presented as the distant end-point which the youthful pupil of wisdom will do well to keep in mind. It sets the parameters for human existence. In consequence claims regarding a new life beyond that of this world cannot be called upon to explain its unresolved and unsettling problems, since what lies beyond death must remain a mystery.

A second point is related to this, since, so far as is practically possible, Qoheleth views death as part of a natural process of life. Not only are there no hints, as in the old Canaanite religion, that death is a monstrous anti-god, threatening and challenging the work of One who is The Living God. Rather Qoheleth tries hard to subsume death as a recognised and inevitable part of the natural order of things. Its inevitability for every living creature is an inescapable fact! The distinction between a living creature and a dead one is therefore a qualitiative distinction which has no counterpart in the whole universe.

So far as Qoheleth is concerned it would not make sense to claim that one pursued the dictates of wisdom 'to avoid the snares of death'. No teaching could make that possible. Death, accordingly, provides the author of Qoheleth with something of a dilemma. On the one hand he shares the insights gained by the earlier wisdom teaching that have 'demythologised' death. It is no longer a fearful power of 'anti-God'. Since it is a part of the destiny allotted to all human beings it must be regarded as a feature of the divinely ordained order of things. It belongs to creation itself and cannot be dismissed as an unfortunate mistake that came into the created order after its inception. It must somehow belong to the intended scheme of things.

Qoheleth, like his predecessors in teaching wisdom, had no insuperable difficulty in accepting that premature death could be a serious misfortune. However such an evil destiny could be regarded as brought on by distortions and neglect of the divine order. What was far more puzzling, and what could not be dismissed by such arguments, was the inescapable fact that all creatures must eventually die as a part of this divine order. For this there could be no simple moral explanation.

In an extended discourse, touching some notes of tragi-
comedy, Qoheleth argues out the thesis that the day of death is
better than the day of birth (Qoh. 7:1-14). However, the
strained arguments fail to provide sufficient support for the
unlikely contention they are put forward to uphold. Every
human instinct is on the side of life, as Qoheleth well realised!
Nevertheless the very boldness of the idea of proposing such a
thesis serves to illustrate Qoheleth's anxiety to view death as a
feature of the order of life. The end result, however, is to
strengthen the feeling that Qoheleth could hide his inability to
resolve such difficulties behind a gentle cynicism. There were
many aspects of human experience which he saw provided a
challenge to the broader claims of wisdom to know all about the
world and the mind of its Creator. For him it was better to
admit the limitations of knowledge than to pretend to a grasp of
truth which failed to correspond to experienced reality.

It is in the early part of the following century that we
encounter the more far-reaching conclusion of the way in
which wisdom had dealt with the problems of sickness and
healing. This is to be found in the teaching of Ben Sira, who
appears as a relatively well to do, and well educated, teacher in
Jerusalem.[24] With him the profession of the physician and
pharmacist has become a fully independent one, no longer tied
to that of the priesthood. No doubt much of this development
was due to the impact of Hellenistic ideas and medical practice
upon Judea. Sickness and illness were too serious a part of
human experience to be neglected, or to be left behind when
new knowledge and understanding were available. Accordingly Ben Sira urges respect for the physician as a practitioner
whose skills were given by God and which bring honour upon
him. At the same time, the very tone of commendation which
Ben Sira adopts strongly hints at the degree of suspicion and
reluctance with which many greeted the physician's skill:

> Have proper respect for the physician, since you have need of him,
> for the Lord established him (in his work); for healing comes from
> the Most High, and he receives his reward from the king.

---

24. Cf. P. W. Skehan and A. A. Di Lella, *The Wisdom of Ben Sira*, The
Anchor Bible 39 (New York: Doubleday, 1987); J. Marbock, *Weisheit im*

The skill of the physician gains respect for him, and he is admired among great men. The Lord created healing herbs from the earth, and an intelligent person will not despise them. Was not water made sweet with a tree in order that his power might be known?

Accordingly God gave skill to human beings that he might be glorified in his wonderful deeds. Through them he heals and eases pain; the pharmacist prepares medicines from them. His works will never be finished; and from him health is upon the face of the earth.

Sirach 38:1–8

The reference back to Exod. 15 makes it plain that Ben Sira was well aware of the longstanding biblical tradition which regarded the non-priestly medical profession with grave suspicion. Undoubtedly the roots of this lay in the close association between much medical practice and the use of incantations and semi-magical rites. Furthermore there was a repeated temptation for non-priestly medical skills to be linked to irregular religious traditions and rites. The deeply-rooted mythological understanding of Baal as the Giver of Life and the Conqueror of Death had no doubt tended to further such suspicion. It therefore suited Ben Sira's purpose, in arguing for due recognition of the independent roles of the physician and pharmacist, to claim that they were simply acting, as Moses had been, as agents and ministers of God's healing power. Their independence of the priesthood in no way implied that they were not truly serving as instruments of God's healing gifts. Effectively therefore Ben Sira's position is that they represented true and proper divinely authorised professions in their own right, which were to be set alongside that of the priest and scribe.

Wandel. Untersuchungen zur Weisheitstheologie bei Ben Sira, BBB 37, (Bonn: P. Hanstein, 1971).

CHAPTER FOUR

Wisdom and Politics

Two features concerning the early origin of wisdom in Israel have a direct bearing upon the relationship which existed between wisdom and politics. The first of these derives from the observation that the influence of Egyptian intellectual and literary pursuits, broadly related to wisdom, was at one period quite strong. Although the Egyptian concept of *maat* is to be understood as 'justice, truth, righteousness, order', rather than wisdom in the precise sense, there are nevertheless a number of important features where the Israelite wisdom's idea of truth and justice overlap with the Egyptian concept.

Such 'justice' (*maat*) was regarded as expressive of an order that pervaded the whole of life. Accordingly the proper functioning of the natural world, the moral order of family life, the upholding of a centrally administered system of law and the structures of state authority by which the royal administration remained in office were all regarded as interwoven and mutually interacting aspects of one ordered whole. Morality therefore could not be separated from politics and the promotion of justice, education and prosperity were all viewed as part of the duty of the ruler to uphold *maat* within his realm. This is very well evident from the earlier Egyptian teaching in the account of a series of petitions brought before the high steward by one who has become known as 'The Eloquent Peasant'. The ideal administrator is portrayed as one who creates a just order of life:

Leader free of greed,
Great man free of baseness,
Destroyer of falsehood,
Creator of rightness,
Who comes at the voice of the caller!
When I speak, may you hear!
Do justice, O praised one,
Who is praised by the praised;
Remove my grief, I am burdened,
Examine me, I am in need!
                    The Eloquent Peasant, 66–71[1]

That such *maat* especially concerned the administration of justice in a court of law is further illustrated from the teaching of Amenemope:

Do not confound a man in the law court,
In order to brush aside one who is right,
Do not incline to the well-dressed man,
and rebuff the one in rags.
Don't accept the gift of a powerful man,
and deprive the weak for his sake.
Ma'at is a great gift of god,
He gives it to whom he wishes.
The might of him who resembles him,
It saves the poor from his tormentor.
                    Teaching of Amenemope, 20:20–21:8[2]

We have followed the historical conclusion that, at an early stage, Israelite wisdom development was strongly affected by knowledge of the aims and characteristics of this Egyptian didactic tradition. Accordingly it is reasonable to accept that something of the same comprehensive understanding of the all-encompassing nature of wisdom began to emerge in Israel during the pre-exilic period. The administrative structures of the state were regarded as an integral part of an extensive order

---

1. Translation from M. Lichtheim, *Ancient Egyptian Literature, Vol. I, The Old and Middle Kingdom*, 1973, Berkeley—Los Angeles—London: Univ. of California Press, p. 172.
2. Translation from M. Lichtheim, *Ancient Egyptian Literature, Vol. II, The New Kingdom*, Berkeley—Los Angeles—London: Univ. of California Press, 1976, p. 158.

which prevailed throughout the cosmos. Consequently the holding of political office and the wielding of political power were understood as part of the grand design of the universe. The king was therefore a divinely appointed agent for organising and imposing a just order upon earth which would embody the requirements of wisdom. Most especially, such a system of wise administration manifested itself in a system of legal administration based on fairness, absence of favouritism based on class or wealth, and in which the king held the highest office.

However it is not only the probability of Egyptian influence which leads us to the conclusion that wisdom in early Israel was directly concerned with what we can broadly describe as the legitimacy and duties of the ruling political powers. A far more decisive and clear-cut basis of evidence exists within the book of Proverbs itself. Here we find a significant number of pieces of sentence instruction which concern the king and his authority. Other items of instruction relate to the duties of lesser officials. Common to all such instruction is the assumption that the king holds office legitimately, that he is to be regarded as an instrument of just order and truth, and that his ability to wield power and to punish wrongdoers are part of a divinely ordained pattern of order.

It has been a part of our attempt to trace the theological development of wisdom in the Israelite-Jewish tradition to argue that the home of the primary wisdom collections which we find in Prov. 10–29 was originally that of the Judean royal court. We can define the teaching contained in this material as representative of the 'old wisdom'. After the catastrophes of 598 and 587 BCE which witnessed the collapse of the Jerusalem court and the destruction of many of its most valued literary assets, the nature of the wisdom tradition changed. It pursued its tasks in a broader and more diversified setting, largely dictated by the fact that there was no longer a single homogeneous national centre of administrative power. Judah could no longer claim to be the exclusive heir of the Israelite tradition and the fact of dispersed Judeans living in many lands had increasingly to be taken into account.

When we recognise the significance of the complexities attendant upon the attempts at restoration of religious and political life in Jerusalem after the collapse of Babylonian control in the region after 538 BCE, we become very strongly aware of the need for a major shift in the very structure of Jewish political thought.[3]

The old political order had established its basis on the claim that a royal covenant existed between the Lord God of Israel and the family of David (2 Sam. 7:1–17).[4] The historical roots and dynastic assumptions of this claim were exclusively Israelite, and essentially Judean, in their nature. After the removal into Babylonian exile of the last survivors of this Davidic family the circumstances arose in which this national frame of reference needed replacement by a more international and universal one. The political sphere required to be grounded in a belief in a universally valid divine order, not that of a nationally focused royal dynasty.

At first it is clear that the main focus of Jewish hopes were centered upon the eventual restoration of the surviving heirs of the Davidic family through the descendants of Jehoiachin (cf. 1 Chron. 3:17–20).[5] Yet these hopes eventually foundered and failed to attain realisation. Probably as significant as this failure was the fact that an increasing number of Jews were content to live in the new lands to which they had been taken, or to which they went in their endeavour to build new lives for themselves. For them the restoration of a Jewish royal house in a country to which they no longer belonged had very limited significance.[6] Much more important were questions of the recognition they

---

3. For the changed political order of the post-538 BCE situation in Judah, combined with the necessity for accomodating the needs of Jews living in dispersion, cf. P. R. Ackroyd, *Exile and Restoration*, (London: SCM Press, 1968), pp. 232ff.; P. D. Hanson, *The Dawn of Apocalyptic*, (Philadelphia: Fortress Press, 2nd ed. 1979), pp. 219ff.; *idem. The People Called*, (San Francisco: Harper & Row, 1986), pp. 263ff.

4. For the centrality of the Davidic covenant tradition in the entire presentation of history in the pre-exilic/exilic historical tradition cf. D. J. McCarthy, 'II Samuel 7 and the Structure of the Deuteronomic History', *JBL* 84 (1965), pp. 131–138 [= *Institution and Narrative. Collected Essays*, Analecta Biblica 108 (Rome: Biblical Institute Press, 1985) pp. 127–134]

5. That the Chronicler wished, and expected to see, a return of the Davidic monarchy whose descendants he so carefully notes, is accepted by H. G. M. Williamson, *1 & 2 Chronicles*, New Century Bible (London: Marsall, Morgan & Scott, 1982), pp. 29–30.

6. Cf. H. G. M. Williamson, 'The Concept of Israel in Transition', *The World of Ancient Israel* (Cambridge: CUP, 1989), pp. 141–162.

were to give to the rulers of the lands in which they had found refuge. The very national frame of reference of the old dynastically based monarchy of Judah disqualified it from providing a suitable focal point for a concept of a divinely willed political order.

There are clear indications that it was the wisdom tradition alone which found itself able to provide the basis for a changed concept of a divine order in the political realm which embraced the new perspectives and realities. This pointed to a universal political order, established as part of the created world, the ideological roots of which were authentically rooted in the Israelite inheritance.

Proverbs of Royal Wisdom

Before considering the way in which a new post-exilic political theology emerged on the basis of the older royal wisdom, it is important to look closely at the kind of teaching that was presented in that courtly wisdom tradition. As we have noted, the older sentence instruction preserved in the book of Proverbs contains a surprising number of items concerned with the wise abilities of the king in the administration of justice.[7] We may note some of the more striking affirmations:

> Oracular decisions are on the lips of a king;
>   his mouth makes no mistake when passing sentence.[8]
>
> Prov. 16:10
>
> It is an abomination for kings to do evil,
>   for the throne is established by right action.
> Truthful lips are the delight of a king,
>   and he loves one who speaks what is true.
>
> Prov. 16:12–13

---

7. Cf. N. W. Porteous, 'Royal Wisdom', *Wisdom in Israel and the Ancient Near East, FS* H. H. Rowley, VTSupp III (Leiden: E. J. Brill, 1955), pp. 247–261 [= *Living the Mystery. Collected Essays,* (Oxford: B. H. Blackwell, 1967) pp. 77–92].

8. Special interest attaches to the fact that the king is here credited with making 'oracular decisions' (Heb. *qesem*). The origins of such a metaphor, since quite clearly the king was not engaging in mantic practices but rather delivering a verdict in a court of law, must lie in the fact that Israelite legal practice resorted to the priestly use of oracular lots where no satisfactory decision could otherwise be reached. Cf. Deut. 17:9. W. McKane, *Proverbs,* pp. 499f. points to 2 Sam. 14:27 for a parallel to the idea.

My son, fear the Lord and the king,
and do not be disobedient to either of them;
for disaster from them will spring up suddenly,
and who knows when their lives will be cut off?[9]

                                              Prov. 24:21–22

We can see immediately a number of features relating to this instruction which are striking. Perhaps most noticeable of all is the affirmation of the pursuit of justice and love of truthfulness which are credited to the king, but which so much of ancient history so patently belies. Secondly we may also sense surprise that ordinary citizens are addressed in a manner which assumes that they have direct dealings with the king. Clearly this can only represent a highly typified situation in which what is being inculcated is essentially respect for the kingly office, as the highest office of state. It is essentially the state itself, and the administration of this through a host of officials working under the king, who are to be respected.[10] The sentence instruction presents in concrete form what, more abstractly, can only be described in terms of obedience to, and respect for, the administrative dictates of the state.

This particularly applies to the first of these sayings concerning the king's inerrant skill in passing sentence on wrongdoers. We are immediately reminded of the remarkable skill in such legal discernment that is credited to Solomon (1 Kgs. 3:16–28). It must be regarded as certain that Israelite kings did not normally spend their time adjudicating in relatively minor legal disputes. Appropriate officials existed for this purpose (cf. Deut. 16:18–20), and, if they could not handle the matter, religious officials were called in to provide a decision on the basis of oracular-divinatory means (Deut. 17:9). The familiarity with such cultic techniques for obtaining oracular decisions has determined the wording of the instruc-

---

9. The past line of v. 22 is obscure and the translation follows that of W. McKane, *Proverbs*, p. 406. It is also of considerable interest for the way in which the wisdom understanding of the political order developed that the LXX translation at this point introduces a much extended series (eleven lines) of sayings concerning the wrath of the king. Cf. G. Gerleman, 'The Septuagint Proverbs as a Hellenistic Document', *OTS* VIII (1950), pp. 15–27.
10. Cf. O. Plöger, *Sprüche*, BKAT XV11 (Neukirchener Verlag: Neukirchen-Vluyn, 1984), pp. 192–3.

tion which places the king's judicial authority at the very highest level of rectitude. He represents the highest court of appeal and the foundation of all administration of justice.

Clearly what is being affirmed here is the authority of the royal administration as a whole. Moreover the last of these affirmations places the king's office on a level with that of God. Just as the decisions of the king are of equal merit as oracular decisions from God, so respect for the king is parallel to respect for God. Accordingly disobedience to the royal office, and all that represents it on earth, is presented as rendering the culprit liable to the most terrible, but rightly merited, catastrophe. In one sense a degree of inconsistency may be recognised in arguing that natural catastrophe will be inflicted on the wrongdoer by God, whereas the judicial authority imposes a punishment by direct human agency. However the argument of the teaching is that the political order which dispenses justice is acting on divine authority.

It is in the light of this that we have to understand the several references to the wrath of the king:

> A king's anger is a messenger of death,
>   and a wise person will appease it.[11]
> In the expression of a king's face there is life,
>   and acceptance by him is like the clouds that bring the spring
>   rains.
> Prov. 16:14–15

> A king's anger is like the roaring of a lion,
>   but his favour is like dew upon the grass.[12]
> Prov. 19:12

---

11. W. McKane, *Proverbs*, p. 488, interprets both vv. 14 and 15 as pointing to the king's anger and his power of preferment or removal from office. This may be so at a surface level, but the repeated concern with the royal anger must surely intend to signify that it expresses the divine anger and is therefore justified. All of these sayings would appear to be about personal actions, only in a very limited way. They are more concerned to show that such personal responses will demonstrate the divine will. R. N. Whybray, *Poverty and Wealth*, p. 54 takes such affirmations as indicating the absolute power of the monarch and the consequent caution that is necessary in dealing with him. This is no doubt true, but the reader is clearly meant to understand that such total power is used justly.

12. McKane, *ibid.*, p. 488, speaks of the king as 'the fountainhead of preferment' and discerns in this saying a consciousness of the royal power of

It is surely not sufficient to interpret such sayings on a purely personal level, since this would be to restrict their applicability to too narrow a circle and would suggest that the king was likely to be an irascible person. Rather the teaching recognises that, as the possessor of supreme power, the king held the ability and the right to do whatever he willed. To suggest that the king was irritable or arbitrary in his judgments would have run counter to the basic assumptions of the wise order that he represented. Rather the aim must be to assert that, because the king stands at the head of a just order, to oppose him and thereby to incur his wrath, is to act against that order so as to render oneself liable to a deserved punishment.

It is in a similar vein that the king's ability to search out and punish misdemeanours is presented as being absolute:

A king who sits on the throne of justice
winnows all evil with his eyes.[13]
Prov. 20:8

A wise king winnows the wicked,
and drives the wheel over them.[14]
Prov. 20:26

The assumption that pervades all these affirmations is that the system of justice which the king maintains, and over which he is the presiding head, is a wholly just and fair system. Clearly we should not for one moment suppose that the authors of such proverbial sayings were presuming to offer advice and admonition to the king. Nor are they trying to be obsequious towards him. Much more fundamental to their aim is the concern to inculcate an acceptance of a social and political order in which the king holds the primary place. This order is a facet of the world-view which the teachers of wisdom claimed to be able to perceive.

---

patronage. Yet the concern lies deeper in suggesting that such royal favour is rooted in the wise order of reality and must be respected.
13. McKane, *Proverbs*, pp. 241, 544f. translates 'winnowing every criminal with his eyes' and comments that 'nothing evades his penetrating scrutiny.'
14. The meaning is rather obscure. Probably the metaphor is of winnowing grain by driving a threshing cart over it. Cf. D. Winton Thomas, *JTS* 15 (1964), pp. 155f., but G. R. Driver, *Biblica* 31 (1952), p. 184, would see here a reference to a 'wheel of fortune'.

It seems highly probable that the somewhat unexpected emphasis upon the ability of the king to search out hidden things, was similarly intended to be especially understood in regard to the royal ability to uncover treasonable plots and seditious activities, and possibly also to root out felons and criminals:

> It is the glory of God to conceal things,
> but the glory of kings is to search things out.[15]
>
> Prov. 25:2

Perhaps here to think of the primary reference in 'searching out' as the investigation and punishment of criminal offences is to narrow the range of meaning too much. A wider range of activities may have been intended, such as the role of the king in the discovery of new knowledge. The evident interest of some branches of the study of wisdom in the observation and classification of the natural world would have been one part of this. The ancient Near East bears ample evidence to the awareness that knowledge and education were not merely a mark of prestige, but also of power and influence. Overall, however, the significant fact is that the king is presented as a supremely wise person. His throne is viewed as established at the top of a social order in which peace, justice, learning and prosperity all have their place.

There are two fundamental features of this portrayal of the king in the older wisdom which deserve attention. Since we have argued that such wisdom was itself composed and collected by circles within the royal court, it would be easy to dismiss such assertions as simply outworkings of a determined and systematic court propaganda. Those who thought so highly of the king were, in effect, thinking highly of themselves, for they held positions, however mean and derivative, by virtue of such a monarchic political system. However this would be to misinterpret the motives and convictions of such teachers. Most basic to their work was the

---

15. McKane, *Proverbs*, p. 579 understands this in the sense: 'The king will never be badly informed or unwilling to take the trouble to get at the truth'. For the king as learned and well informed cf. also R. N. Whybray, 'The Sage

assumption that they, and the king whom they served, were all servants of a divinely given order of life in which wisdom, justice and social order needed to be upheld. If they were to fail in their duty, they would be offending against the very wisdom they believed pervaded all of life.

It is noteworthy that the earlier teaching of the wise in pre-exilic Israel is conscious that individual rulers may not live up to the ideal that wisdom expected of kingship as an institution. Consequently we find condemnation of oppressive kings indicating that tyranny is out of keeping with the nature of the royal office in society:

> It is an abomination to kings to do evil,
> for the throne is established by righteousness.
>
> Prov. 16:12

> Like a roaring lion or a charging bear
> so is a wicked ruler lording it over the poor.
>
> Prov. 28:15

> A ruler who lacks discernment heaps up oppression;
> but he who hates graft will enjoy a long reign.[16]
>
> Prov. 28:16

> When righteous persons wield authority, people rejoice;
> but when a wicked person rules, they groan.[17]
>
> Prov. 29:2

In spite of this warning that individual rulers may act in an oppressive and tyrannical fashion, the older wisdom appears to have nothing to say concerning their right to rule. It regards the right of office which the king enjoys as proper and beyond question, even though the king may act in a manner unworthy

---

in the Israelite Royal Court', *The Sage in Israel and the ANE*, eds. J. G. Gammie and L. Perdue, pp. 133 ff.
16. For the translation cf. McKane, *Proverbs*, pp. 255, 629f.
17. Cf. McKane, *Proverbs*, pp. 256, 639. That the Old Testament contains, in all the main branches of its writings, a considerable body of criticism of kingship as an institution is a marked characteristic of its political thinking. Not only do prophets, such as Elijah and Elisha, appear as sharp critics of individual kings, but the wisdom writers also adopt such a stance at several points. Cf. F. Crüsemann, *Der Widerstand gegen das Königtum*, WMANT 49, Neukirchen-Vluyn, 1978. K. W. Whitelam, 'Israelite Kingship. The royal

of that responsibility. No questions are raised as to who is going to be king, or in what circumstances it might be proper to remove him from office. The fact of monarchy is taken for granted as the most basic of all human social institutions. Accordingly the authority of the one who sits on the throne of the kingdom is regarded as unassailable and divinely given. We shall see that this was a point that was not regarded as so inevitably unquestionable and divinely sustained in Israel, any more than it has been in other nations.

Solomon as Wise King

The connection between wisdom and kingship in ancient Israel found its strongest expression in the belief that Solomon had been a supremely wise king. The claim that this was so is presented in a series of narrative tales which serve to draw attention to his wisdom and which illustrate its outworking. A great deal of scholarly discussion has arisen in an effort to trace back the historical roots of this tradition and to understand what factors led to its creation.[18] Many historians have remained sceptical whether any very firm historical basis can be adduced to explain this claim that Solomon was a supremely wise ruler. Others have been less doubtful, but have remained convinced that, whatever the basis of its historical origin, the tradition fits rather awkwardly with the memory of a king who undoubtedly did much to weaken the kingdom which he inherited from David.

Our concern in the present context is neither to attempt a fresh evaluation of the historical evidence for Solomon's claim to wisdom, nor to consider other possible explanations which encouraged a later age to fasten onto the figure of Solomon and

---

ideology and its opponents', *The World of Ancient Israel*, ed. R. E. Clements, pp. 119–140.
18. For the origin of the tradition that Solomon was the leading patron and source of wisdom in Israel see my essay 'Solomon and the Origins of Wisdom in Israel, *Perspectives in Religious Studies*, 15 (1988), pp. 23–36; J. L. Crenshaw, *Old Testament Wisdom*, pp. 42–54; W. Brueggemann, 'The Social Significance of Solomon as a Patron of Wisdom', *The Sage in Israel and the Ancient Near East*, pp. 117–132; R. N. Whybray, *Wealth and Poverty*, p. 46, n. 1.

to credit him with great wisdom.[19] Rather it is to note how the traditions which ascribe great wisdom to Solomon illustrate the importance of the connection between wisdom and monarchy as an institution.

We may distinguish four such narrative reports concerned to affirm the unique gift of wisdom that Solomon possessed. The first of these in 1 Kgs. 3:3–15 is the most forthright and pietistically extreme in what it affirms. It reports how, on an occasion when the king went to offer sacrifice in Gibeon, he received a revelation of the Lord in a dream by night. In this dream the king was offered from God any gift that he desired. In response Solomon asked for the gift of wisdom since, by implication, this was the attribute that was most needful for one who would be ruler of a great people. God is then pleased that Solomon has asked such a gift and assures the ruler that he will receive not only this wisdom, but also riches and honour such as no other ruler possessed in Solomon's lifetime.[20]

From the perspective of our present concern the main interest lies in the manner in which the gift of wisdom is defined in Solomon's request:

'Give your servant therefore an understanding mind to govern your people, that I may discern between good and evil; for who is able to govern this your great people?'

1 Kgs. 3:9

This quality of judicial insight into right and wrong is then further reinforced by the Lord's response:

'Because you . . . have asked for yourself understanding to discern what is right, . . .

1 Kgs. 3:11

Clearly the kind of wisdom that is envisaged is primarily the

---

19. As, for example, R. B. Y. Scott, 'Solomon and the Beginning of Wisdom in Israel', *Wisdom in Israel and the Ancient Near East*, pp. 262–279, who finds in Prov. 25:1 evidence for believing that the age of Hezekiah was a primary occasion for the growth of a connection between Solomon and Israelite wisdom.
20. For this tradition cf. K. A. Deurloo, 'The King's Wisdom in Judgement. Narration as Example (1 Kings iii), *OTS* XXV (1989), pp. 11–21.

insight into ethical and moral issues which will enable the king
to administer a system of just and fair laws. It is essentially
juridical wisdom that is requested. The character of the story as
a piece of royal propaganda is evident, and it is clearly the kind
of anecdote which might have been told of many rulers. Its
unexpected attribution to an event that occurred at the
sanctuary of Gibeon has been occasioned by the primary
position that it has been given in the reports of Solomon's
reign. Coming, as it does, before the temple had been built in
Jerusalem this location was felt to be acceptable. Similarly its
familiarity with the cultic practice of nocturnal incubation in a
sanctuary in order to receive a dream revelation places it rather
on the margins of the wisdom tradition. In its extreme belief in
royal virtue it stands closer to the popular traditions of folklore
than to the mainstream teaching of wisdom. So too does the
belief that wisdom could be acquired by a supernatural
endowment, rather than by the patient industry of careful
observation and self-discipline. In many respects, therefore, it
savours more of popular kingly folklore than of basic concern
with the nature of wisdom. However it is significant on account
of its affirmation that a close bond existed between wisdom and
juridical administration. It serves well as a basis for promoting
the claims of a royal court to establish a system of legal
administration.

The second of the tales of Solomon's wisdom in 1 Kgs. 3:16–
28 acts as a wholly appropriate sequel to the story of the dream-
vision. In this the king is shown exercising deep psychological
insight into the competing legal claims on the part of two
prostitutes. When each claims to be the mother of a child,
Solomon is able to see that true mother-love would rather part
with the child than see it harmed. Like the story which
precedes it, it too displays several folklorist motifs and it is only
its recognition that true wisdom in legal matters requires what
we should define as 'life-experience' which makes its attribution to Solomon significant. Its inclusion at this point in the
story of Solomon's reign must rest in part on the popularity of
the motifs it contains and its ability to demonstrate the way in
which a system of law can protect the innocent, while
condemning the guilty.

The third of the reports of Solomon's wisdom is found in 1 Kgs 4:29–34 at the end of a list of the major state officials which Solomon's administration introduced. It is important on account of the extent of the recognition that it gives to the fact that wisdom was a pursuit of many nations, and that it was especially nurtured in Egypt. It is also striking on account of the character of the wisdom which is ascribed to Solomon, which is of a very different order from that ascribed to him elsewhere:

> He also uttered three thousand proverbs; and his songs were a thousand and five. He spoke of trees, from the cedar that is in Lebanon to the hyssop that grows out of the wall; he spoke also of beasts, and of birds, and of reptiles, and of fish.
>
> 1 Kgs 4:32–33

Important historical implications may be present in this report. However, for our concern with the character of royal wisdom its main significance lies in the way in which it associates the kingly office with learning and education. The political importance of this in antiquity should not be overlooked. The need to provide a body of trained officials to run the machinery of state, such as the preceding lists describe, was itself a reason for promoting schools of learning and accounting. Such a formal system of education was largely tied to the royal courts of antiquity and clearly ancient Israel was no exception.

We should also bear in mind the likelihood that it was important for the royal administration to seek to limit certain skills and activities to those who were supportive of the established government. Education was itself a means of access to power and influence, so that, as in many of the European courts of more recent times, the interest shown by royal personages in education served as a means of securing the established order.[21]

---

21. Cf. W. Brueggemann, 'The Social Significance of Solomon as a Patron of Wisdom', p. 132: 'Royally formed knowledge inevitably serves royally valued interests'. Cf. also J. L. Crenshaw, 'Education in Ancient Israel', *JBL* 104 (1985), pp. 601–615; M. Haran, 'On the Diffusion of Literacy and Schools in Ancient Israel', *Congress Volume Jerusalem* 1986, VTSupp 40, 1988, pp. 81–95.

The last of the sequence of tales aimed at presenting a picture of the great wisdom of Solomon is found in 1 Kgs 10:1–25 and concerns the visit of the Queen of Sheba to hear the king's wisdom and to see his great wealth. Like the first two such stories of Solomon's wisdom, it bears many folklorist traits and has been celebrated as such in the extent of its popular elaboration in subsequent biblical interpretation.[22] However its major contribution to our understanding of royal wisdom lies in the manner in which it relates the possession of such wisdom to the achievement of prosperity and fame. The wise are presented as those who have expectations of great prosperity and advancement in this world and, since this wisdom is allied to the monarchy, the wisest of kings must surely have achieved the greatest prosperity and fame.

Overall, when we consider the implications of these stories concerning Solomon's wisdom they illustrate further the picture that we have already obtained from the sentences concerning the office of the king in the book of Proverbs. They place in the centre of the claim to royal wisdom the king's role as the head of the administration of justice. Clearly this was a foremost goal for the development of kingship as an institution. Next to retaining control of the military forces in the kingdom, the king asserted his authority most directly over the lives of his citizens by imposing a system of justice through officials, and systems of law, which he established. Such a juridical system, although presented as divine law, and possibly based on wider traditions of 'common law', were administered throughout the ancient East by officials appointed by the king. In this Israel was no exception, although many of the earliest historical developments are still not clearly traceable.

The concomitant aspects of royal wisdom, its responsibility for learning in an international setting and the promotion of trade for increased prosperity, were also not unimportant ways in which wisdom was associated with the royal court. Seen in a larger ancient Near Eastern context, it becomes clear that ideas of wisdom were very closely related to the institution of

---

22. Cf. E. Ullendorff, *Ethiopia and the Bible*, Schweich Lectures 1867 (London: The British Academy, 1968), pp. 131ff.

monarchy and provided a broad intellectual framework for the development of law and education as functions of the state.

Wisdom and the Ideology of Kingship

So far our study of wisdom and politics has pointed to two major conclusions. First among these was the recognition that the political order was viewed as a very important aspect of a more comprehensive cosmic order. The king acted as the agent of God to bring a just and beneficent social order on earth. In a very special way this duty to promote and uphold the structures of a divinely conceived wise order of life placed the king at the very centre of the human concern with wisdom. For a society built on a monarchic system of government, it was, of necessity, proper to regard the king as the wisest of men, and one who held office by God's own choice.

Both in the sentence instruction of the book of Proverbs and in the stories of Solomon we have encountered a close relationship between wisdom and kingship focused upon the portrayal of the king as an individual human being. In reality, however, it is important to recognise that Israel's kingship was not simply the product of the personal charisma of its founders, but represented an aspect of a wide-ranging cultural and political development of the ancient world. Kingship was at the head of a very extensive system of economic, social and administrative developments which changed the entire political contours of antiquity. The economic basis for these developments lay in agriculture and the promotion of trade between cities and communities. Literacy and the invention of techniques of accounting and commercial negotiation provided a means of enhanced capital ventures. In turn these required a body of trained officials and the resultant increased prosperity made possible new expectations of leisure and the emergence of a relatively wealthy middle class. Society became more prosperous, more able to express interest in artistic attainment, and more diversified, as the gap between the rich and the poor became more marked. At the same time new social alignments emerged as the ranks of the commercial middle class established links between themselves and similarly successful persons of other nations. Wisdom could flourish in an international setting.

All of this points towards the conclusion that kingship was immensely significant to the ancient world, not simply for the type of political power structure that it introduced, but for the larger range of cultural attainments which it made possible. The social institution where all these changes found expression was the city as the major centre of human activity.[23] It is not suprising therefore that the proponents of wisdom should have come to look upon the city as the natural arena of success or failure:

> When righteous persons do well, a city rejoices;
>   and when the wicked perish there are shouts of delight.
> By the blessing of upright persons a city is exalted,
>   but it is ruined by the speech of wicked men.
>
> Prov. 11:10–11

Such teaching is of relevance to understanding the importance of the link between kingship and wisdom, since it marks a further example of the way in which kingship formed the apex of a great pyramid of social change and development. In a not inconsiderable measure the pursuit of wisdom provided much of the intellectual stimulus and rationale for such changes. It is no doubt true that there had existed an older stratum of folk wisdom in the world from which Israel emerged. However, whatever links there may have been between such folk wisdom and the more sophisticated learning of the circles linked to the royal court, it is the latter which has come to predominate in the biblical tradition.[24] Wisdom became part of the 'new culture' which thought highly of the state and its officials;

---

23. Cf. F. S. Frick, *The City in Ancient Israel*, SBLDS 36 (Missoula: Scholars Press, 1977); Dom C. Benjamin, *Deuteronomy and City Life*, (Lanham: Univ. Press of America, 1983).

24. R. N. Whybray, *Wealth and Poverty*, pp. 54f. points out that overt mention of the king and of court activities does not prove that such instruction originated in a court setting, since a popular regard for the king could infuse much wider teaching. However, it is not simply a popular estimate of kingship that is presented in such teaching. Rather the king is placed in a fully pivotal role in the entire structure of society and it is this fact which shows that a major ideology of monarchy is being affirmed. Since this

which viewed with enthusiasm the possibilities of commerce and capitalist ventures between cities and nations and which abandoned the inherent suspicion of foreign influence in favour of a greater degree of international exchange. Wisdom was part of an 'enlightened' way of life, even though such a way was only open for a relatively small educated *élite* to pursue.

We have noted, however, that the close link between wisdom and politics finds its strongest expression in the Old Testament in the claim that Solomon was the wisest of all kings. Yet the extreme way in which this claim is presented, elaborated with popular folk-tale like stories, arouses suspicion as to its historical veracity. It is a case of protesting too much. Since Solomon is presented as having been so wise and successful, then it must be because there existed in Israel a deep feeling that he was, in reality, an oppressive tyrant. Indeed the aftermath of this king's reign, besides some aspects of his achievements, demonstrate this very clearly. The stories of Solomon's great wisdom serve as a form of apologetic for a ruler who had left a legacy of division and great bitterness. Whereas the stories concerning both Saul and David illustrate that both these individuals possessed a considerable measure of personal charisma, especially in military exploits, Solomon lacked any such tradition of commendatory personal fame. Instead he has been credited with the more conventional, but most kingly, of all charismatic gifts, that of wisdom.

The reason for this apologetic is easy to trace, for it is on account of Solomon's position as the son and chosen successor of David that his positive attainments as a king are defended. All the more has this become necessary, since the memory of a large united kingdom, which survived only for the brief period in which David and Solomon reigned, provided a picture of the 'ideal' political structure of Israel.

It is also evident from the apologetic nature of the narratives which recount the manner of Solomon's birth and succession to the throne, that serious questions were current within the nation concerning the legitimacy of both events! Solomon was a controversial figure whose reign had done much to cloud the

had real difficulties in establishing itself in ancient Israel, the provenance of such teaching in court circles appears to me to be extremely probable.

reputation of kingship as a form of government. The stories of his great wisdom therefore, whatever the historical veracity and nature of their origin, have been employed to bolster the reputation, not simply of Solomon as a historical figure, but more directly of the continuing divine legitimacy of the Davidic dynasty of which he was a member.

It was the refusal of Rehoboam, his successor in Jerusalem, to alleviate the oppressive measures imposed by Solomon which resulted in the defection of the larger part of Israel from submission to the Davidic kingly rule. They also gave rise to deepened opposition to the very institution of kingship as a whole, as Samuel's warning in 1 Sam. 8:10–18 makes plain.[25]

This is of great significance for understanding the changes that occurred in the teaching of wisdom regarding the political office of the king after the ending of the Judean monarchy in 587 BCE. In the pre-exilic period it did not come within the purview of wisdom to resolve questions of by what right a particular dynasty should retain power upon the throne. Nor was it within the scope of the older wisdom to resolve the inevitable competing claims of various members within that royal family as to who should be king.

The basic issue of the divine right of the Davidic dynasty to provide, in perpetuity, kings over Israel was recorded in historical tradition and ascribed to the prophet Nathan (2 Sam. 7:1–15). It was thereafter celebrated as a basic given datum of the Jerusalem cultus (Pss. 2, 45, 89, 110, 132 etc.). Only after the catastrophe of 587 BCE, when the Davidic dynasty had been removed from power in Jerusalem, did the question of a wider appeal to wisdom as underscoring the value and divine appointment of kings take on a new significance.

Wisdom and Politics after the Catastrophe of 587 BCE

In 587 BCE the last surviving king of the Davidic line, Zedekiah, was removed from office by his Babylonian conquerors and, after witnessing the death of his sons, taken as a prisoner to Babylon. He apparently died there not long afterwards.

---

25. Cf. my essay 'The Deuteronomistic Interpretation of the Founding of the Monarchy in 1 Sam. viii', *VT* 24 (1974), pp. 398–410.

However his nephew Jehoiachin had already earlier been taken to Babylon as a hostage and kept as a prisoner and was able to establish a not unimportant family there. From this ex-king and his sons there emerged a strong hope that, before too long an interval, this royal family in exile would return to Jerusalem and would provide once again a ruler upon the throne in that city. As events transpired such a hope was never to achieve realisation, although, once Babylonian rule collapsed in the face of new Persian conquerors, there was a major revitalisation of it.[26] It appears to have remained a major part of Judah's hoped-for programme of restoration for some considerable time after the Persian Empire took control of Judah and its affairs.

Why this hope foundered in the late sixth century BCE, and how its failure was greeted by a majority of Jews, whether those resettled in Judah or those who had established new homes for themselves in various parts of the Persian empire, remains a historical mystery. What is clear is that such a hope retained a certain latent power and was not wholly abandoned. Rather it was shelved for a more favourable political situation to emerge. More significantly still, it seems highly probable that this hope was itself a divisive issue among Jews in the new situation that had arisen with Persian sovereignty.[27] Very probably the necessity for reaching a compromise political agreement which was acceptable to the Persian authorities could entertain no place for such a restored monarchy on the throne in Jerusalem. It is the advocacy of such a compromise political arrangement which we find set out in the programme of reforms undertaken by Ezra and Nehemiah, themselves both products of the new world of diaspora Judaism.

It is against such a background that we can best understand the major shifts in the ideology of kingship which occurred at this time. Best known and recognised among these shifts was the retention of the royal monarchic ideal in the form of a 'messianic' hope to be attained at some unspecified time in the

---

26. Cf. P. R. Ackroyd, *Exile and Restoration*, pp. 124f.
27. For evidence of strong conflicts and political dissension in Judah cf. P. D. Hanson, *The People Called*, pp. 253ff.

future.[28] The basis for this hope was nurtured by earlier prophecies of the greatness of Israel attendant upon the Davidic monarchy, especially those preserved in the book of Isaiah. It seems probable too that the retention of so many royal psalms from the pre-exilic period served to keep alive the hope that the Davidic monarchy would, at some stage, be restored.[29] It may well have been the case that this postponement of the expectation of restoring a monarchy was itself intended to act in rather contradictory directions. Whereas it kept alive such a hope for a future time, it also provided adequate justification for shelving such an expectation in the present, since to attempt to implement it would have provoked the necessity for taking unacceptable political decisions.

In any event it is apparent that this hope of restoring the monarchy after the catastrophe of 587 BCE became a dormant one. It has been plausibly suggested that it was also substantially modified by being regarded as a symbolic promise that pertained to Israel as a whole, and did not require an actual reigning monarch.[30]

However there was a very different approach to the question of the future of monarchy in the post-exilic life of Judaism which is of considerable importance. This emerged as a development of the earlier wisdom contention that kingship was a structural part of the wise and beneficent order of life that pertained throughout the cosmos.

In the long speech in Prov. 8:1–31, delivered by the personified figure of wisdom, her role in the order of creation from the very beginning is heavily stressed. The goodness of the natural world, the order of human society and the ability to achieve wealth and happiness are all ascribed to wisdom. Wisdom is the principle of goodness and harmony that pervades all things, providing a cement that binds the natural and the moral worlds together. It is within this order that we find the bold affirmation:

---

28. Cf. S. Mowinckel, *He That Cometh*, ET G. W. Anderson, (Oxford: B. H. Blackwell, 1956) pp. 280ff.; J. Becker, *Messianic Expectation in the Old Testament*, ET David E. Green, (Edinburgh: T.&T. Clark, 1980) pp. 58ff.
29. Cf. my essay, 'The Messianic Hope in the Old Testament', *JSOT* 43 (1989), p. 14.
30. Cf. J. Becker, *Messianic Expectation*, pp. 68ff.

By me kings reign,
and rulers decree what is right.
by me statesmen exercise rule,
and nobles govern justly.[31]

Prov. 8:15–16

In much of what is affirmed here we are face to face with similar teaching about the relationship between wisdom and monarchy to what we have learnt from the pre-exilic period. Almost certainly, however, this new teaching is post-exilic in its origin. It asserts the political role of wisdom, not simply from within a national context, but quite explicitly in an international setting. Monarchy itself is a political institution that is necessary to the order of creation. Hence it is recognised as necessary for the whole world, not, as with Solomon and the Davidic dynasty, simply as a part of the divine order for Israel. It is more extensively seen as necessary for all nations. It is therefore regarded as wholly appropriate that submission to such kings and princes is right, no matter what their national origin. The political power structures of international society are affirmed as lying in accordance with wisdom, because they are the power structures that exist in the real world and are responsible for administering justice and good order.

Clearly, in presenting such teaching on behalf of wisdom, there can have been no intention of claiming that all kings were noble and just. Already we have seen that wisdom fully ackowledged that bad rulers betrayed the purposes for which their office existed. Nevertheless, what is provided here is a clear theological mandate for the recognition of the right of kings to rule, even when they were not rulers of Israel's own approved royal dynasty. Nor indeed is it required that they should be worshippers of Israel's God. They form part of a wise cosmic political order that has been ordained since creation itself.

It is recognisable that something similar to such teaching is already to be found earlier in sayings attributed to the great prophets. The book of Jeremiah insists that God has ordained

---

31. The Hebrew has '—all of them are righteous rulers', which may be correct, but the emended text presupposed here has received wide acceptance.

that 'all the earth' should submit to the power of Nebuchadnezzar (Jer. 27:12–15). Isa. 45:1–6 asserts that Cyrus has been
chosen and empowered by the Lord God to fulfil a purpose
directed towards Israel. Now the expanded wisdom teaching of
the post-exilic age has broadened out its teaching concerning a
cosmic order to embrace the kings and rulers of all nations.

It is not difficult to see how important this teaching was for
the political stability and development of Judaism after 538
BCE. Clearly the exilic age, as expressed through its prophetic
hopes for Israel's restoration, had envisaged that Israel would
once again become a nation among other nations.

It was within such a context that the hope of restoring the
Davidic heirs to the throne in Jerusalem made eminent sense.
Kingship was a badge of nationhood. Yet it was not to be!
Under Persian rule Jews had to learn to live as citizens of many
nations. In fact, under Persian control, it is evident that the old
concept of nationhood had only a very limited validity.
Successively Assyrian, Babylonian and Persian rulers had
striven to weaken the national ideal in the hope of promoting
thereby the power and strength of their own imperial order.
Jews had to come to terms with this reality and it is evident that
their ability to do so was in no small way a basic feature of their
survival and ability to flourish and to develop their religious
and cultural life.

It is in this new political situation that arose after 538 BCE
that the willingness of the teachers of wisdom to recognise that
kingship was a necessary, and potentially righteous and
beneficent, institution was very significant. Jews did not need
to abandon their ancestral religious loyalty in order to
acknowledge the right and authority of rulers who were neither
native Israelites nor worshippers of their deity. All kings were,
at least in the ideological foundations of their office, 'ordained
by God'. It was right therefore to render them obedience and
honour.

It is not difficult to see that there were evident limits to this
obligation of submission to non-Jewish rulers and state
officials. Potential dangers existed which are highlighted in a
popular and partisan fashion in the book of Esther and which
broke out with great violence in the Maccabean revolt.
Nevertheless, it becomes evident that the willingness of the

scattered Jewish communities which established themselves in dispersion under Persian and Greek rule to acknowledge foreign rulers was a major step in securing the future of their life and faith. It was eventually also to become important for the growth and success of the Christian Church which drew upon it.

The Limits of Royal Power

Perhaps it is not surprising that the teachers of wisdom have not left us any very clear discussion of what limits might be set to this recognition of kingly authority, if it became threatening towards Jewish religious life. Almost invariably the defence of the traditional forms of Israelite-Jewish religion, when they were threatened by hostile political actions, became centred upon the cultus and its officials. The trend of the teachers of wisdom was, however, to look rather in the opposite direction of making ideological accomodations and establishing a sense of an overarching providential order which operated among all nations. The relative warmth with which wisdom eventually embraced many features of Hellenism is ample testimony to this trend.

However there existed within the wisdom tradition a strong awareness that injustice and tyrannical oppression were contrary to the office of the king as ordained by the order of creation.[32] This feature is increasingly elaborated in the later wisdom teaching, leading to some unresolved questions of political loyalty and suggesting a measure of 'quietist' submissiveness which evidently strained the credibility and patience of many Jews.

Such a resigned acceptance of aspects of monarchy which were unpalatable is well shown by Qoheleth:

> Keep the king's command, and do not be afraid on account of your sacred oath; if a matter becomes threatening, go from his presence hurriedly, for he does whatever he pleases. For the word of the king is supreme, and who may say to him, 'What are you doing?'
> Qoh. 8:2–4

---

32. Such criticism of oppressive kingship is found in Prov. 28:15; 29: 4, 12. Cf. Whybray, *Wealth and Poverty*, pp. 53f. This may well be of pre-exilic

What we are faced with here is not merely an observation concerning the potentially dangerous nature of absolute monarchs, but an underlying theology of statehood in which the king held the supreme position. This power is assumed to be wholly legitimate, even though there is some awarenesss that absolute power is dangerously corruptible.[33] Since by Qoheleth's day few Israelites were likely to encounter the king in any direct personal fashion, it seems probable that what is set out here was intended to be understood more widely and to be applicable to all those who held office by royal commission.

The awareness that, through the seeming oddities of dynastic privilege and historical changes, unsuitable and unworthy persons might become rulers is fully recognised:

> Woe to you, O land, when your king is a child,
>   and your princes feast in the morning!
> Happy are you, O land, when your king is the son of free men,
>   and your princes feast at the proper time,
>   for strength and not for drunkenness!

Qoh. 10:16–17

The emphasis here is placed on the unworthy behaviour of rulers, although the picture of a child-king indicates a sensitivity to the effects that dynastic privilege could produce. There is, however, an even sharper awareness by Qoheleth of the violent changes that could take place in the political realm:

> Folly is set in many high places, and the rich sit in a low place. I have seen slaves on horses, and princes walking on foot like slaves.

Qoh. 10:5

If we are to place Qoheleth in the second half of the third century BCE, then his political and social reflections here would seem to be aimed at testing the inherited teaching of wisdom against his own historical knowledge and experience. Nothing at all appears to be left of the older popular belief, associated with Solomon's name, that a ruler might be granted

---

origin, but does little more than indicate that individual kings may fail to live up to the demands of their office.
33. Cf. J. L. Crenshaw, *Ecclesiastes*, p. 149; R. N. Whybray, *Ecclesiastes*, NCB, pp. 130f.

exceptional wisdom as a divine gift. Similarly the idea of any divine right to rule is lost sight of when set against the rise and downfall of particular rulers, a feature that fits well the internal factions and fightings of the Ptolemaic age. Although Qoheleth still appears to maintain the belief that kings reign through the operation of a divinely determined providence, the modes of working of this providence are shown to be inscrutable. His teaching on the subject of kingship therefore can scarcely be regarded as continuing to provide a reasoned account of the nature of political authority as a foundational part of a wise order of the world. Rather the reader is encouraged to accept the irrationality and inscrutability of the actual political order, however serious its defects, since this is taken, in spite of appearances, to be the order given by God. His motto, therefore, is 'Do not expect to understand everything in the world, least of all the political world!'

This attitude of acceptance of tyranny and submission to the arbitrariness of the political order of the world is carried further in the teaching of Ben Sira:

> Many kings have had to sit upon the ground,
>   but one who was never thought of has worn a crown.
> Many rulers have been greatly disgraced,
>   and illustrious men have been handed over to others.
>   Sirach 11:5–6

This awareness of the unpredictability of life, and the consciousness that experience did not demonstrate that a principle of rational and traditional right upheld the political order, is taken as indicative that life should not be presumed upon. The very arbitrariness and unpredictability of the political realm is applied in a moralistic fashion to illustrate a quite different, but undoubtedly deeply rooted, feature of wisdom's teaching. This concerned human inability to control all affairs of life, with a consequent necessity for maintaining a humble and unquestioning acceptance of the supremacy of God's ordering of all things.

Ben Sira appears also to have been anxious to note further the contradictions of experience that had attracted the attention of Qoheleth. The inherited claims of wisdom affirmed that God maintained a providential hand upon the powers of government upon earth, directing them towards the maintenance of a just and beneficent social order. Experience, however, posed many challenges to this and allowed the usurpation of political control by persons who were quite unworthy to be rulers. At the same time, the widespread acceptance of forms of traditional authority based on dynastic privilege, often led to the holding of power by weak and unprincipled rulers:

> An undisciplined king will ruin his people,
>   but a city will grow through the understanding of its rulers.
> The government of the earth is in the hands of the Lord,
>   and over it he will raise up the right man for the time.
> Sirach 10:3–4

In some attempt to defend the notion that God keeps a very direct hand upon the ordering of political life, Ben Sira invokes the old wisdom concept of God's intolerance of tyranny and human pride:

> The Lord has cast down the thrones of rulers,
>   and has seated the lowly in their place.
> Sirach 10:14

It is in a similar vein that the mystery and arbitrariness with which a person may be stricken with illness is used to support the idea that an element of unpredictability pertains in all human life. To an extent this is a problem with which the book of Job wrestles. Such misfortune may then be used by God to bring down the mighty from their thrones:

> A long illness baffles the physician;
>   the king of today may die tomorrow.
> Sirach 10:10

Overall in the teaching of wisdom concerning the political realm we can discern some striking and important developments and shifts. From the earliest preservation of a literary record of the teaching of wisdom in Israel it appears that its connection with the institution of kingship was prominently recognised. The king belonged within the order of society which wisdom endeavoured to serve. That an older folk wisdom may have preceded this has certainly to be taken into account, but even in this it seems likely that the king was looked up to, however idealistically, as an especially wise person. It is this link between wisdom and monarchy that has led to the powerful focus of attention upon the figure of Solomon as the wisest of kings.

After the downfall of the Davidic monarchy in 587 BCE, however, another aspect of wisdom's teaching about the political realm was set in the forefront. This viewed all kingship as part of a wise ordering of the world since the days of creation. All kings could be seen to have a place in such an all-encompassing cosmic order.

This provided an important platform for Jews to build upon in their need to establish a more subtle form ₁f political theology to take acount of the more complex situation of those living in dispersion, or even those living in Judah under the overall sovereignty of Persian rule. Its ability to achieve this, and to retain a substantial measure of moral and religious uniqueness, while accepting the legitimacy and divine ordering of this foreign domination, must be regarded as a great intellectual success for the wisdom tradition. It brought out a far more workable and constructive political theology than could possibly have been achieved by the older cultic ideas and mythology of kingship. These remained tied to the traditions of the Davidic family and survived after the downfall of that dynasty in the form of an elaborate, and often politically dangerous, form of messianic hope.

In the Hellenistic era, when faced with the injustices and flagrant abuses of political power by the new masters of Judah, the rather idealistic nature of the teaching of wisdom about kingship came under increasing strain. This strain is fully evident in what both Qoheleth and Ben Sira have to teach upon the subject. At the same time as seeking to defend the fundamental assumptions of wisdom about the nature of kingship as part of a divinely planned order of the cosmos, these later writers fall back upon an appeal to submit to the inscrutability of the workings of providence. In an effort to make this more palatable they reiterate the compensating idea, which also had its place in the older wisdom teaching, that wrongs are sometimes righted with great suddenness and that even the most vigorous and powerful of human beings may experience sudden catastrophe.

CHAPTER FIVE

Wisdom and the Household

Any concern with the theological and ethical ideas which came to the forefront in the wisdom literature of ancient Israel must take account of the kind of society for which that literature was written. Since an evident desire to persuade and to educate motivates the composers of the admonitions and instructions of the wise, we must necessarily be concerned to clarify the setting in which such guidance was offered. It might readily be assumed that the social background which the teachers of wisdom regarded as normal for those whom they sought to guide and instruct was simply that which pertained generally for Israel throughout its long history in the biblical period. Although there may be some measure of truth in such an assumption, we must recognise that it is very far from explaining the situation with any precision.

We need, in any case, to take acount of the immense scale of the social, political and economic changes which took place in Israel and Judah throughout this period.[1] From being a community of loosely allied tribes, in which the kinship

---

1. The importance of the changing concepts of community in the Hebrew Bible are well shown in P. D. Hanson, *The People Called. The Growth of Community in the Bible* (San Francisco: Harper & Row, 1986). Awareness of the larger Gentile world as a context for divine presence and action are set out as 'Witness to an alternative Vision', pp. 312ff. It is argued here that the post 587 BCE development of the wisdom tradition also presents its own understanding of community which became of immense importance to the early Christians.

structure of the clan and the extended family was paramount, it became for a brief period a single nation. This subsequently split into two separate sister kingdoms both of which eventually collapsed under the pressure of Mesopotamian imperial expansion between the eighth and sixth centuries BCE. Later, and only briefly, did Judah regain a recognisable degree of national identity in the second and first centuries BCE.

By this time there were many widely scattered Jewish communities settled more or less permanently outside the borders of Judah. These maintained a strong and firmly identifiable religious life of their own. In total numbers they undoubtedly exceeded the sum of those living within the borders of Judah. Moreover, in Judah itself the population was far from being homogeneous. The Jewish people had largely become a collection of separated religious communities with a central point of focus in Jerusalem and its temple.

We have argued that it was especially in this period when the international dispersion was becoming the established pattern of Jewish life, that wisdom came to fulfil a special educational and spiritual role. We do not discount that there was a much older tradition of folk-wisdom rooted in the kin structures of the ancient Israelite clans, since there are some signs of a survival of this. Also we have adhered to the view that, during the period of the divided monarchies, aspects of the wisdom of the ancient Near East, particularly that of Egypt, began to penetrate into Jerusalem court life. Accordingly, wisdom became for a period the cultured expression of diplomatic and social skills appropriate to a royal court.

When the last remnants of Judah's national state administration collapsed in 587 BCE wisdom came to be especially nurtured and promoted as an instrument of education and spiritual guidance for the growing number of scattered Jewish communities. The very breakdown of the central political and religious institutions of the temple and the royal court necessitated the promotion of more flexible, and individually fostered, ways of maintaining the Israelite–Jewish tradition.

We have described this state of affairs as one of liminality, drawing upon the valuable insights of Victor Turner regarding the stresses, gains and insights concomitant upon a 'betwixt and between' period of upheaval and change. Old values and allegiances were dropped and replaced by new ones. New patterns of social bonding took place and new opportunities were embraced. A new freedom was found, while old loyalties were mourned and lost. In some respects wisdom became a 'transitional philosophy', maintaining identifiable links with the past, but adapting them to new ways and conditions.

This whole experience of Jews living in their dispersed communities came to be regarded as merely a transitional phase, until a return to a single national reality could again be realised. Such an overall perspective on the changed situation after the Babylonian exile is made abundantly clear in fundamental attitudes adopted in the prayer life of the period (cf. especially the remarkable prayers of Ezra 9; Neh. 9; Dan. 9).

So much that is characteristic of the wisdom tradition of the Old Testament, especially as it is found in the Book of Proverbs, reflects both the tensions and originality of this distinctive attitude to life. The cult, with its technical language and mythological world-view, is seen from a distance. It is respected but looked upon as lying outside the purview of both the wisdom teacher and his pupils. Just as strikingly the royal house and the royal court are spoken of with great respect and approval, but are no longer tied to a national historic covenant and a specific royal dynasty.

We must ask then what were the primary institutions which the teachers of wisdom regarded as foundational for the life of Jews who remained loyal to the tradition of 'the fear of the Lord'?[2] The answer to this lies in the recognition of a threefold layering of the community. At the most basic level was the household. This centred upon, and apparently usually sheltered, the family unit. Outside of this lay the city which provided the broader horizon of the community and the basis of its security and prosperity. Beyond this lay the less firmly shaped concept of the nation.

---

2. That the Jewish wisdom tradition evidences a distinctive view of the Jewish social world has increasingly drawn the attention of scholars. Cf. R. Gordis, 'The Social Background of Wisdom Literature', *Poets, Prophets and Sages. Essays in Biblical Interpretation* (Bloomington: 1971, pp. 160–197);

The Centrality of the Household

Christopher Hill has described the Puritan conception of the home as 'the Spiritualization of the Household'.[3] Our Puritan forefathers derived this understanding of the Christian household from their reading of the Bible, and it is clear that the Book of Proverbs is a primary source where such a comprehensive picture of the spiritual structure of the individual pious home was found. It was the wisdom teachers of ancient Israel who developed in a most distinctive and forthright fashion a doctrine of the importance of the household as a place of piety and education. This devolved upon the primacy of the father as the head of the house, the responsibility of both parents for instruction of their children, and the necessity for these children to be obedient to their parents and to give careful heed to what they were taught. This wisdom teaching promised, as a consequence of such a spiritual home structure, the assurance that the household would be the sphere of 'blessing' and that it would be secure and would prosper.

It is therefore a prominent feature of the teaching of the wise of the Old Testament that the household is regarded as the most basic and primary functioning unit of the community. Consequently we find repeatedly in the wisdom admonitions a concern to preserve its unity and integrity. Such individual households were seen to constitute the primary economic units within the community so that the prosperity of individuals was dependent upon the prosperity of the household in which they were resident. At the same time such capital as a family acquired became part of the inheritance which was kept within the household family unit.

Before looking in more detail at what the wisdom teachers had to say about the spiritual stucture of the household, and how they sought to buttress its social and economic strength, it is useful to consider something of the reasons which brought about this shift away from the large extended family, with its

---

R. N. Whybray, 'The Social World of the Wisdom Writers', *The World of Ancient Israel*, ed. R. E. Clements, (Cambridge CUP, 1989), pp. 227–250.
   3. C. Hill, *Society and Puritanism in Pre-revolutionary England* (Harmondsworth: Penguin Books, 1986), pp. 429–466.

clan and tribal affiliations, to focus upon the individual household.[4]

The significance of Christopher Hill's comments upon the way in which the English Puritans of the seventeenth century sought to spiritualize the life of Christian homes is of relevance. Hill points out that a prominent reason for doing so was because they wanted to make the home a powerful centre of Christian nurture and education. By achieving this they could offset the inherent tendencies of a traditional pattern of piety focused upon churches and the ordained priesthood. The home became the primary place of prayer and religious education because the sanctuaries and their clergy were not, in Puritan eyes, wholly to be trusted.

Some features of this situation are analogous to those which pertained to Jews living in dispersed communities away from Jerusalem. Even after the temple was rebuilt and rededicated in 516 BCE an increasing number of loyal Jews had to maintain their faith without physical opportunity to participate in its worship. At the same time as this physical separation from the solely authorised place of Jewish worship developed, the political confusion which followed upon Judah's collapse in 587 BCE led to the break-up of the large, territorially based, families and clans of old Israel. Individual families became broken up and the traditional land-holdings which had served to bind the extended family together were denied to them. With the removal of the monarchy there took place a major dislocation of the economic and political system in which the kingship had played the dominant role.

A return to the stability and ordered structure of the pre-587 BCE situation became a feature of the widely expressed hope of Israel's recovery of its status as a full nation. In turn such a restoration of Jewish nationhood became the central goal of a prophetic hope which intruded into all aspects of public and private prayer. Israel was living 'between the times', with the

---

4. An instructive and valuable survey of these developments is outlined by G. E. Mendenhall in 'The Relation of the Individual to Political Society in Ancient Israel', *Biblical Studies in Memory of H. C. Alleman*, eds. J. M. Myers, O. Reimherr, H. N. Bream (Locust Valley N.Y.: J. J. Augustin, 1960), pp. 89–108; cf. also *ibid.*, 'Social Organization in Early Israel', *Magnalia Dei. The Mighty Acts of God. FS G. Ernest Wright*, eds. F. M.

old nation destroyed and the new one not yet born! Meanwhile
life had to be lived, and worship had to be encouraged, within
the circumstances which the ruined state of Judah and the rise
of the dispersion allowed.

The very emphasis upon genealogy and ethnic descent which
begins to permeate Jewish life from this period reflects the
realisation that kinship and the cohesion of the large extended
family could no longer be taken for granted. Judaism had
become a varied mixture of communities settled among other,
frequently hostile, Gentile communities. The internal tensions
engendered by this, where the traditional obligations and
loyalties of the extended family were frequently neglected, is
well illustrated in the story of the Book of Ruth. Contrastingly
the external pressures exerted by Gentile neighbours is well
shown up in the Book of Esther. It is probably not by chance
that the heroine in each of these stories is a woman, since it
appears evident that the emphasis upon the individual
household, and the loss of the protective support of the the
extended family, placed increased responsibilities upon the
Jewish woman.

Accordingly the Jewish family unit had come largely to be
definable in terms of those who lived within a particular Jewish
household. This is well brought out in the wisdom affirmation:

.   Grandchildren are the crown of the aged,
      and the glory of sons is their fathers.
                                                 Prov. 17:6

It is striking that the concept of brotherhood, which is
otherwise very highly regarded in early Israel as among the
most powerful of kinship ties, appears not to have provided the
wisdom teachers with a concept which carried with it a high
sense of obligation. In fact rather the reverse is true since, as we
shall see, the experience of friendship and neighbourliness
provided a social bond which was regarded more highly than
that of brotherhood.

The Jewish households which the admonitions and instructions of the wise presuppose are recognised for the most part to

Cross, W. E. Lemke and P. D. Miller, Jr. (Garden City: Doubleday, 1976),
pp. 132–151.

belong to a city, in the safety and prosperity of which each member household was benefitted:

> When life goes well with the righteous, the city rejoices;
> and when the wicked perish there are shouts of delight.
> Prov. 11:10

> By the blessing of the upright a city is honoured,
> but it is ruined by the talk of wicked persons.
> Prov. 11:11

The integrity and good order of each household was therefore seen to be a matter of importance to the larger city which provided its main social arena.

It is in line with this focus upon the individual household that it is regarded by the wise as the most essential 'school' and place of education. In some cases it appears that it is the head of such a household who is addressed in the teaching, but more frequently he is prevailed upon to act as teacher. In some instances clearly the mother is urged to share in such teaching (Prov. 1:8), while in a very notable instance the instruction given is uniquely credited to a royal mother figure (Prov. 31: 1–9).[5]

It is probable that some parts of the Book of Proverbs contain teaching relating to the life of a professional, or semi-professional, class of scribes and advisers (cf. Prov. 23:1–12).[6] There must certainly have been some schools where a more formal pattern of education, including some professional training, was available. Such special tuition had to be paid for (cf. Prov. 17:16), and no doubt the skills of literacy and rhetoric were of paramount importance, and were not cheaply to be obtained. Nevertheless, in spite of all the clues and hints which point to the elements of a formal educational system having developed in Israel and Judah,[7] the primary context of the teaching of wisdom that is to be found in the Book of Proverbs is that of the home. This broad domestic context of

---

5. Cf. J. L. Crenshaw, 'A Mother's Instruction to Her Son (Proverbs 31: 1–9)', *Perspectives in Religious Studies* 15 (1988), pp. 9–22.
6. Cf. A, Lemaire, 'Sagesse et écoles', *VT* 34 (1984), pp. 270–281.
7. Cf. J. L. Crenshaw, 'Education in Ancient Israel', *JBL* 104 (1985) pp. 601–615.

the collected wisdom teaching of the book also conforms to the observation that it bears all the marks of having been intended to be taught, and responded to, by all sections of the Jewish community. It is aimed at a broad, community-wide, response, not a narrow professional one. Its appeal is to everyone who has the sense to listen, and to heed, its warnings.

We can therefore confidently work on the assumption that, in the Book of Proverbs, it is the individual non-priestly Jewish household that is accorded the most central role in the teaching of wisdom. Neither the central sanctuary of the temple, nor the administratively influential royal palace and its attendant bureaucracy, appear as more than distantly functioning realities. The primary sphere of moral responsibility and social action is the individual household of relatively small family groups.

It is when we look closely at this canonical tradition as represented in the book , that we are struck by the fact that the household has become such a primary unit of society. Hill describes it in Puritan teaching as 'the lowest unit in the hierarchy of discipline',[8] and this fully echoes its role in biblical wisdom.

The Household as the Primary Sphere of Blessing

What we have argued for in regard to the social context of the Jewish wisdom teaching is not that it has abandoned the importance of kinship as a source of value and moral obligation. Rather such obligations derived from loyalties of kinship have become modified by a new emphasis upon the individual household. In the pre-exilic morality of Israel the extended family had assumed the major role in enforcing discipline, exacting revenge, and, where necessary, protecting the interests of weaker members of the family group. In the understanding of the wise, however, these obligations and supports based on family links are almost entirely subsumed under the notion of the household. Admittedly those who live

---

8. C. Hill, *Society and Puritanism*, p. 429.

within the household are recognised as a kin-group, but it is to this household that loyalty is due.

It is then no surprise that, by elevating the status of the household in this fashion, the teachers of wisdom celebrate this as the sphere where good or evil prevail. The individual household effectively displaces the cult as the sphere of blessing. Repeatedly we find such a viewpoint openly asserted:

> The house of the wicked will be destroyed,
>   but the tent of the upright will flourish.
>   Prov. 14:11

Wisdom serves to maintain the household, whereas the rejection of wisdom leads to its collapse and destruction:

> Wisdom builds her house,
>   but folly with her own hands tears it down.
>   Prov. 14:1[9]

This enjoyment of blessing makes the house of the family that heeds the teaching of the wise a place of prosperity:

> In the house of the righteous there is much treasure,
>   but trouble befalls the income of the wicked.
>   Prov. 15:6

In the introductory poems to the Book of Proverbs which set out the broad principles of the teaching of the wise we find a summarising presentation of the basic doctrine:

> The Lord's curse is on the house of the wicked,
>   but he blesses the abode of the righteous.
>   Prov. 3:33

So the household is presented as the unit of society in which prosperity can take effect and where security is provided. It is the sphere where the consequences for good or evil of adherence to, or rejection of, the principles of wisdom are most

---

9. NRSV reads 'The wise woman builds her house . . .' cf. note; also W. McKane, *Proverbs*, pp. 231, 472.

readily to be seen. Because the household is the protective
umbrella which covers the closely-knit kin-group, the prosperity of the righteous household establishes the basis of
prosperity and security for future generations:

> A good man leaves an inheritance to his grandchildren,
> but the wrongdoer's wealth is laid up for those who act rightly.
>   Prov. 13:22

The Good Neighbour

If we follow up the clues provided by our outline sketch of the
social background in which the written wisdom of the Old
Testament was primarily developed, then we are immediately
given a basis for understanding one of its primary features.
This concerns its great attention to the role of the 'neighbour',
or 'friend', since the same Hebrew word (*re'*) is variously
translated as one or other of these in most English versions of
the Bible. As the loyalties and duties attendant upon affinities
of kinship, beyond the immediate family circle, no longer
provide the most keenly felt set of principles for action, so,
contrastingly, the fact of living in proximity to others is exalted
to provide some of the most far-reaching of all. Neighbourliness, not brotherliness, is the watchword of the teachers of
wisdom! A good neighbour, who is a true friend, is more worth
having than an unreliable brother:

> A friend loves at all times,
> and a brother is born for times of trouble.
>   Prov. 17:17

> There are neighbours who pretend to be friends,
> but there is a friend who is more reliable
> than a brother.
>   Prov. 17:24

The primary identifying characteristic of who this
'neighbour–friend' might be, is that he, or she, is someone who
lives close to the person addressed. J. Fichtner defines the
'neighbour' quite simply as 'someone of the immediate
neighbourhood with whom a person comes into contact

through daily life, through living as a neighbour, through working together, or through casual meeting.'[10]

The overall importance for the development of biblical ethics of what we find here cannot be overlooked. The teachers of wisdom have come to recognise the moral priority of the household, comprising a single family unit, as the basis of Jewish society. When set alongside this the wider obligations of kinship and family ties, which had earlier formed so central a part of the basic ethical duties of ancient Israel, are of lesser significance.

No doubt with their longstanding attachment to ideas of 'blood–revenge' (cf. 2 Sam. 3:22–30, esp. the curse of v. 29), and their propensity for long-lived vendettas, the ties of kinship could often become dangerous and corrupting. Perhaps even more frequently they proved a hindrance to right moral action through the ability of wealthy and influential families to distort the course of justice (cf. Exod. 23:1–3). Set against this kinship-oriented morality the teachers of wisdom sought to give priority to a far simpler basis of human relationships. The simple fact of living and working in close proximity to other persons established duties of obligation and respect towards them as fellow human beings.

It is certainly the case that such fellow citizens are assumed to be Jews, but it is the fact of living in the same neighbourhood, and not belonging to the same family, that provides the central point for establishing a bond with them. It is also of significance that it is the same word which can denote one who is both 'neighbour' and 'friend', since there is a strong concern on the part of the wise to insist that the person who listens to their advice will take good care to turn his 'neighbours' into 'friends'.

The extensive range of teaching concerning the building up and maintaining of good relationships with the persons who

---

10. J. Fichtner, 'Der Begriff des "Nächsten in Alten Testament" ', *Gottes Weisheit*, Arbeiten zur Theologie II.3 (Stuttgart: Calwer Verlag, 1965), p. 95; D. Kellermann, *TWAT*, VII, 545–555; J. Kühlewein, *THAT*, II, 786–791; C. Burchardt, 'Nächstenliebegebot, Dekalog und Gesetz in Jak. 2, 8–11', *Die Hebräische Bibel und ihre zweifache Nachgeschichte. FS R. Rendtorff*, eds. E. Blum, C. Machholz, E. W Stegemann (Neukirchen–Vluyn: Neukirchener Verlag, 1990), pp. 517–534.

constitute such 'neighbours' of the wise makes it impossible to
do more than to note its chief characteristics. Although the
precise meaning of the Hebrew is rather obscure, the message
of Prov. 22:11 appears to be that, a person of good intent and
gracious speech could even have the king as his friend:

> Those who have a pure heart and
>   are gracious in speech
> will have the king as a friend.
>   Prov. 22:11 NRSV[11]

Although the translation is uncertain the notion of 'the
friendship of the king' would appear to be a hyperbole
designed to express the idea of enjoying the esteem of even the
highest members of society. In urging a right attitude towards
one's neighbour therefore the wise had much sound advice to
offer. Clearly for a start it made good sense that one should
never despise (or 'belittle') those who are one's neighbours
(Prov. 11:12). Nor should the intelligent person invent
malicious charges against them (Prov. 24:28), or attempt to win
them by flattery, which would quickly be seen through (Prov.
29:5).

The one reason why neighbourly behaviour might become
difficult is, rather instructively, recognised to rest in economic
matters:

> The poor is disliked even by his neighbour,
>   but the rich person has many friends.
>   Prov. 14:20; cf. also Sirach 13:15–20

> Wealth brings many new friends,
>   but a poor person is deserted even by his friend.
>   Prov. 19:4; cf. Sirach 18:13

> Many seek the favour of a generous man,
>   and everyone is a friend to a person who gives gifts.
>   Prov. 19:6

---

11. The Hebrew of Prov. 22:11 is particular difficult and LXX is very
different. McKane, *Proverbs*, pp. 245, 576f., translates:
  'A king loves a man with a pure mind
  the grace of his speech meets his approval.'

This social division caused by the disparity between wealth and poverty is further commented on in Prov. 19:7. More than any other factor it is felt that the division between rich and poor makes a difficult bridge for neighbourliness to cross. Simply showing kindness towards the poor, which the wise appear strongly to advocate, merely reinforces the sense of separation between them. It may indeed be precisely such a point that the teachers of wisdom wished to draw attention to, since the fact of wealth and poverty raised deep questions about the Creator's purpose (cf. Prov. 14:31; 19:17).[12]

The complex question whether it could be wise to take one's neighbour to court is hinted at in Prov. 25:9-10, although perhaps the admonition here is more directly aimed at keeping any quarrel or disagreement with a neighbour as a private matter. To air the matter publicly, or to try to get others involved, would only make matters worse. Furthermore it would run the risk of bringing disgrace back on the head of the person who thought to give his neighbour a bad reputation.[13]

Overall there is much wise advice about using commonsense in establishing neighbourly relationships. 'Do not be too frequent a visitor to a neighbour's house' is the advice of Prov. 25:17; nor should one put oneself under a financial obligation towards a neighbour which could strain the relationship and turn an erstwhile friend into an enemy (Prov. 6:1-5).

Even when a neighbour is seen to be acting badly, there are reasons why it might be best to say nothing about it:

> Do not be in a hurry to go to law
> over what your eyes have seen,
> for what will you do afterwards,
> when your neighbour humiliates you.
> Prov. 25:7c-8[14]

It can undoubtedly be interesting and instructive to follow

---

12. Cf. P. Doll, *Menschenschöpfung und Weltschöpfung in der alttestamentlichen Weisheit*, SBS 117 (Stuttgart: Verlag Katholisches Bibelwerk, 1985).
13. Cf. W. McKane, *Proverbs*, pp. 250, 581f.
14. The translation 'to go to law', follows the Hebrew text and seems the most probable meaning. Cf. O. Plöger, *Sprüche Salomos*, pp. 294ff. However the Greek of Symmachus read as 'to bring to the multitude; i.e. to publicise widely. The warning would then be against vexatious litigation, or, as Plöger

through the wide range of warnings and advice that the wise of ancient Israel preferred on the subject of learning to be a good neighbour. However, from the overall perspective of the theology of wisdom, the striking feature is that the concept of the 'neighbour' has become such a prominent one. The interaction of social change, moral conscience and theological conviction has brought about a very fundamental shift in the recognised foundations of moral action. No longer is it the conventional and immensely powerful obligations of kinship which are to control one's behaviour. Rather it is the simple fact of living and working together that determines action.

The Primacy of Parental Instruction

It is against this background in which the household is exalted to such a prominent position that we can best understand a number of features which have tended to characterise the aims of biblical wisdom. Prominent among these we must set the great emphasis that is placed upon the duty of parental instruction and the need for careful attendance to it. This is set in the very forefront of the introductory admonitions of the the proverbial wisdom, since the entire strategy of attaining wisdom's goals depends upon it:

> Hear, my son, your father's instruction,
>   and do not reject your mother's teaching;
> for they are a beautiful garland for your head,
>   and pendants for your neck,
>
> > Prov. 1:8–9

> Hear, you children, a father's instruction,
>   and be attentive, that you may gain understanding;
> for I give you good rules:
>   do not forsake my teaching.
> When I was a child with my father,
>   youthful and beloved in the sight of my mother,
> he taught me and said to me,
>   'Set your mind to remember my words;

---

suggests, against jumping too readily to conclusions when the situation is not properly understood. McKane, *Proverbs*, pp. 580f. favours following the Greek tradition.

keep my instructions, and enjoy life;
do not forget, and do not turn away from what I say
Get wisdom; get insight.

Prov. 4:1–5

My child, keep your father's commandment,
and do not let go of your mother's teaching.
Keep them in your mind always;
tie them about your neck.

Prov. 6:20–21

Several features are noteworthy, not the least being the importance that is attached to heeding the instructions of both the father and the mother. Education is a function of the home and is a responsibility shared between both parents. Nor can we fail to recognize the close similarity between the language used to reinforce the injunction to heed this parental instruction, which is described as composed of 'commandments' (Heb. *ḥuqqim*), and the language of the *shema'* (Deut. 6:4–9). This fact lends strong support to the contention[15] that the formulation of the Ten Commandments has itself been heavily influenced by the tradition of 'clan wisdom'. There is, however, a further factor which merits consideration and which highlights the relevance of the parallel between the development of wisdom in ancient Israel and the rise of a Puritan ethic in seventeenth century England. Hill points out that the Puritan concern with the spiritual authority of parents was directly related to the reduced authority of priests in the post-Reformation era. This would appear to have had a close parallel in post-exilic Judaism. In Jewish communities, experiencing the necessity for establishing and upholding a strong central religious tradition, in increasing measure at a distance from the temple and its priesthood, the resources of wisdom were developed to meet this need. Since wisdom was primarily a lay expertise, with roots in the family life of small clans and affinities with a central governmental administration, it could appeal to the parental authority that operated within the household-group. This provided a form of natural, and

---

15. Cf. E. Gerstenberger, *Wesen und Herkunft des 'Apodiktischen Rechts'*, WMANT 20 (Neukirchen-Vluyn: Neukirchener Verlag, 1965) pp. 61ff.

widely recognized, authority as well as an effective medium for imparting doctrine. It is noteworthy too that it could make appeal to the rational need for maintaining and preserving the integrity of the family as an economic unit.

We should note that serious questions have been raised whether the address in the Book of Proverbs to the pupil as 'son' and the definition of the teacher as 'father' are to be taken at their face value. In a society where the principle of kin-relationships was so readily accepted, it is arguable that it would have been natural for any teacher to have assumed the role and title of 'father'. The usage itself therefore would not, of itself, prove that an actual parent was necessarily the agent of the teaching. In this case we could consider that the teaching took place in a school setting, rather than the home. However the fact that both parents are sometimes referred to as fulfilling this teaching role very strongly points to the recognition that it was the pupil's natural parents that were involved. This is further supported by the strong inference that the 'house', or 'tent' as it is sometimes described archaically, formed the location for such activity and provided the sphere where a positive response to it would most markedly bear fruit. Furthermore the attention to the need for physical punishment, if admonition alone did not succeed, and the warnings of the attendant dangers if the son refused to show obedience, all point to actual households as the location where wisdom instruction was given. It is basic religious and moral instruction, but, as in the case of Puritan teaching, it discounts any priestly involvement altogether.

Because of this central importance that was attached to the role of parents in teaching wisdom to their children we can best understand the level of seriousness that is attached to this process of education. It could be set in the relatively bland terms of a recriminatory statement:

> A fool despises his father's instruction,
>   but he who heeds admonition is prudent.
>   Prov. 15:5

> Whoever loves discipline loves knowledge,
>   but he who hates reproof is stupid.
>   Prov. 12:1

Yet reproof and reprimands clearly did not always achieve the desired result so that sterner measures were required, tempered by an ultimately good aim:

Discipline your son while there is hope;
   do not set your heart on his destruction.
                        Prov. 19:18

Blows that wound cleanse away evil;
   strokes make clean the innermost parts.
                        Prov. 20:30

He who spares the rod hates his son,
   but he who loves him is diligent to discipline him.
                        Prov. 13:24

The familiar teaching of Prov. 22:6 also belongs to this setting:

Train up a child in his proper way[16]
and when he is old he will not depart from it.

It is against such a background that we can see the great importance that was attached to obedience and the inculcation of a strong consciousness of family and household commitment in children:

A wise son makes a glad father,
   but a foolish man despises his mother.
                        Prov. 15:20

A stupid son is a grief to a father;
   and the father of a fool has no happiness.
                        Prov. 17:23

A foolish son is a grief to his father
and bitterness to the woman who gave birth to him.
                        Prov. 17:25

We are not simply being faced here with a modest sense of satisfaction that children should follow in the steps of their

---

16. The Hebrew is difficult, but this appears to be the correct meaning. The reference is to that way of life which is most beneficial to the youth.

parents. More was at stake, for the household had a pivotal role to play in the stability and structure of society as a whole. Divided and unstable households quickly became economically weak, and there was clearly little room for slackness and laxity. A household which had members who failed to fulfil the obligations that fell naturally to them was unlikely to be economically strong enough, or socially influential enough, for its position in the community to be maintained. We can fully understand therefore why there is this note of undoubted sternness and urgency that was attached to the teaching concerning the responsibilities of children towards their natural parents. It was the household as the foundational social unit that was threatened when offspring refused to heed the instruction given to them. In this regard we may claim that the goal of such teaching was not simply to ensure adherence to a specific set of rules for the good of society in general, but more directly to ensure among children a positive and fixed attitude of life which placed the household in the forefront of its concerns.

The Contentious Wife and the Erring Husband

Set in the light of this primary importance that is attached to the household as the centre of social life, we can better understand the great importance that is attached to two other aspects of the teaching of the wise. The first of these is the sharp, and seemingly chauvinistic, concern with the troublesome and contentious woman.[17]

First of all we find enunciated a broad general principle which we may take to have been applicable to all members of a household:

> Whoever makes trouble for his household will get nowhere
> (literally 'will inherit wind'),
>   and the fool will become servant to the wise.
>
>   Prov. 11:29

This sets out clearly the point that we have contended for:

---

17. Cf. especially C. V. Camp, *Wisdom and the Feminine in the Book of Proverbs*, Bible and Literature Series 11 (Sheffield: Almond Press, 1985).

the household was the umbrella of the family who lived under its protection. To preserve its harmony and psychological wellbeing, as well as its economic viability, was a matter of prime importance for all its members. There was, correspondingly, little emphasis upon what we should describe as a purely personal and individual set of life goals. The individual's expectations of personal achievement and success were heavily circumscribed by those of the household to which he, or she, belonged. Accordingly actions had to be tempered to fit in with this goal.

Very specifically we find a number of items of sentence instruction which point to the contentious woman as a source of trouble in the household:

> It is better to live in a corner of the housetop
> than in a house shared with a troublesome woman.
>
> Prov. 21:9

> It is better to live in a desert land
> than with a troublesome and ill-tempered woman.
>
> Prov. 21:19

We may suppose that usually such a woman who is referred to was the wife and mother, but clearly this was not always the case. Grandmothers, or even unmarried daughters or sisters, may often have been the culprits. We are at first inclined to regard such teaching as either pointing out an obvious fact which has become the source of a class of humour, or alternatively, as making a rather laboured point out of a feature of life which applies in many other contexts as well. Contentiousness and quarrelsomeness are not limited to male-female relationships. However, the prominence that is given to the issue in the wisdom teaching needs to be understood as a further reflection of the strong concern that it displays to maintain the integrity and solidarity of the household.[18] There

Claudia Camp points out (pp. 250ff.) the immense importance of family integrity for the economic security of the household.

18. The question of the status of wives in the early Israelite family, as reflected in legal formulations, has been much discussed. Cf. C. J. H. Wright, *God's People in God's Land* (Exeter: Paternoster Press, 1990) pp. 183ff. Overall the very attention to the role of the woman as wife and mother in the wisdom literature appears to represent a considerably

are therefore correspondingly positive affirmations concerning
the immense blessings of a happy marriage:

A good wife is the crown of her husband,
  but a woman who brings disgrace is like disease in his bones.
                                                        Prov. 12:4

These sayings are rescued from belonging to the category of
the obvious and the overly mundane since they gain their force
and weight from the importance that was attached to
maintaining the solidarity and harmony of the household as a
social unit.

There is then a closely related feature of the wisdom teaching
which focussed attention upon repudiating the wayward male
who went after other women and who thereby brought shame
and disunity to his own home. It is evident that admonitions
addressed to young men against succumbing to the seductive-
ness of the immoral woman play a surprisingly prominent role
in Prov. 5–9. In fact the portrayal of wisdom as a beautiful and
virtuous young woman in Prov. 8:1–36 is best understood as an
artistically planned counterpart to the picture of the immoral
woman of Prov. 7:1–27. Similarly the closure of the Book of
Proverbs with its description of the virtues of the good wife and
mother of Prov. 31 would appear to have been motivated by the
desire to place the issue of marital loyalty and 'homebuilding'
as a central concern for wisdom.

A measure of uncertainty attaches to the particular social
status of the women whose wiles are so sharply condemned. In
Prov. 7:6–27 she appears clearly to be a prostitute, and this is
also true of the 'foolish woman' of Prov. 9:13–18. On the other
hand the 'evil woman' and 'adventuress' of Prov. 6:24 is
apparently an adulteress, and not a prostitute (Prov. 6:26), and
this may well also be the case with the immoral woman whose
ways are repudiated in Prov. 5:1–23. As Claudia Camp has
argued in her persuasive study of these admonitions, they
appear to highlight the point that Jewish households of the
early post-exilic era felt themselves to be particularly threat-

---

enhanced status accorded to her. She was seen as a pillar of the home on
which so much of its prosperity and happiness rested.

ened by youthful sexual adventuring and by a husband's infidelity to the marriage bond.[19] It is noteworthy too, in view of the attention that feminist issues in biblical literature have been accorded in contemporary scholarship, that it is the waywardness of the husband that is primarily the point of attention. The addressees of these homilies are clearly male.

Our concern here is not to raise again some of the complex issues relating to Old Testament attitudes towards the sexes. Nor yet is it to question again whether there may not lie behind the teaching of Prov. 5–9 echoes of an older goddess cult in which some forms of cult-prostitution may have been practised and which the authors of the wisdom teaching were concerned to suppress.

All such concern with the possible prehistory of the material appears to be highly speculative and is in no way a necessary inference to be drawn from what is set out. Once we recognize the central role that wisdom accorded to the household, and the way in which this appears to have been especially highlighted in the early post-exilic period, then the material can be fully understood. For wisdom the household had become both a school and a spiritual training ground. It was also the unit of economic viability which maintained its potential strength through well established rules of inheritance. The need to uphold a sense of household responsibility found its expression in this concern for the preservation of the family. To do this had become a matter of primary importance to Jewish religious and social survival. This was evidently true in all historical and political settings, but never more so than in the particular environment presented by life in the Jewish diaspora. What had been a natural part of Israelite community life in the pre-exilic world of existence as a nation, became a matter of utmost urgency to maintain in the harsher post-exilic world of many small, politically subservient, enclaves of Judaism.

This centrality of the household in the life of ancient Judaism can be understood from three related points of view: economic, social and psychological. From the economic point of view, it is apparent that wealth was primarily held within

19. C. V. Camp, *op. cit.*, pp. 227ff.

families. Undoubtedly families could and did collaborate for mercantile enterprise, but, in general, the wealth of the family head was held for the benefit of the whole family, and, correspondingly, any debts or financial failures became the responsibility of the entire household. The prevalence of a system of debt-slavery made this negative aspect a very threatening feature of life, with child-slavery a very common factor. Alongside of this we can see that normally the family served as the primary unit for the alleviation of poverty and the prevention of starvation, whether this was caused by debt, accident or other social misfortune.

On the broader social front the family was of central significance since it is evident that concepts of honour, and its contrasting counterpart shame, attached most directly to families and households, rather than to specific individuals. A person acquired standing in the larger social context of town and country through the household to which he, or she, belonged. Accordingly actions which weakened this, or which brought it into disgrace, served to undermine the acceptability in the community of all its members. All the members of a household could thereby suffer when one of its members brought it into debt or brought shame upon it.

On the third front, that of psychological wellbeing, we encounter another, and rather unexpected, feature of the teaching of the wise. They insisted that the individual required inner peace and contentment in order to achieve a satisfactory standard of life. In many respects this is one of the particularly intriguing features of what it had to offer. Violent emotions, constant stress, or even a morose temperament, could undermine personal happiness and make life a painful experience thereby defeating the aims of wisdom. In all the goals that the wise set for the attainment of the good life their recognition that among them an inner peace was important, reveals their genuinely spiritual nature. To this extent they can truly be said to have set a goal for the 'spiritualisation' of the household.

Looked at against such a background it is wholly under-standable that for female members of a household to make it a place of contention and disturbance was strongly condemned. So also acts of sexual adventuring, however casual, by male members were sharply repudiated since they also threatened the integrity and social standing of the family and the household. in which it was located.

The Blessing of Work

There is a further aspect of the Old Testament wisdom teaching which has frequently been noted, and where a striking shift in theological thought is evident. This concerns its powerful doctrine of work:[20]

> He who farms his land will have plenty of food,
>> but he who follows worthless pursuits has no sense.
>>> Prov. 12:11

> The hand of the hard-working will rule,
>> while the lazy will be put to forced labour.
>>> Prov. 12:24

So important was this necessity for an active and industrious way of life thought to be that it is urged that it should take precedence over personal comforts and concerns:

> Prepare your work outside,
>> get everything ready for yourself in the field;
>> and after that build your house.
>>> Prov. 24:27

That this emphasis upon work was among the least popular aspects of the wisdom teacher's themes of admonition is suggested by the fact that it is sometimes put humorously and with a measure of poetic embellishment:

> I passed by the field of a lazy person,
>> by the vineyard of someone without sense;
> and look, it was all overgrown with thorns;
>> the ground was covered with nettles,
>> and its stone wall was broken down.

---

20. Cf. R. N. Whybray, *Wealth and Poverty in the Book of Proverbs*, pp. 31f.

Then I saw and reflected upon it;
    I looked and received instruction.
'A little sleep, a little snooze,
    a little quiet relaxation,'
then poverty will leap upon you like a robber,
    and destitution like an armed man.
                                        Prov. 24:30–34

The rendering of Prov. 12:9 is very much in dispute. The RSV takes as:

Better is a man of humble standing who works for himself
    than one who plays the great man but lacks bread.

This translation follows the ancient Greek, and Plöger still regards it as possible.[21] However NRSV translates as:

Better to be despised and have a servant,
    than to be self-important and lack food.

If the Greek has the correct sense it would suggest that the wise regarded it as particularly important to retain the opportunity for profitable work in one's own hands, rather than to become dependent on others for its rewards. However, most modern interpretations find in this admonition a warning against going hungry in order to create an imposing social impression.[22] If this is so, it is difficult to see why retaining a servant, who could not readily be afforded, was regarded as so important. The saying is best interpreted as establishing a contrast between engaging in work, however menial, which guarantees food, and going hungry in order to keep up appearances.

---

21. O. Plöger, *Sprüche Salomos*, p. 146. Cf. also REB: 'It is better to be modest and earn one's living, than to play the grandee on an empty stomach.' The sense would then be that it is better to have a trade and work, rather than starve for the sake of keeping up appearances. Cf. Sirach 11:11–13.
22. W. McKane, *Proverbs*, pp. 229, 444 renders it as: 'A man of small means with one servant is better off than one who makes a show of grandeur but is short of bread'.

Clearly the wisdom teaching on this particular front has a very close connection with the substantial teaching that the wise had to offer on the subject of wealth, its acquisition, its use and its hazards. In general the wise viewed with the gravest suspicion any attempt to get quick and easy money. Wealth needed to be earned, and the school of life had shown that this was not usually achieved by risky, or hastily planned, ventures or harsh and oppressive attitudes. Money had to be gained honourably, usually slowly and with difficulty, and had then to be used wisely and, where possible, built up into an inheritance.

Of all the sections of the Old Testament literature it is the wisdom writings which reveal most about the social impact of a moneyed economy upon Jewish life in the ancient world.

What is particularly striking is the contrast that emerges when we compare this emphasis upon the wisdom instruction relating to the necessity for work with the older cultic concept of blessing. In essence we may claim that no fundamental disagreement is present, since the cultic language concerning blessing and prosperity must itself necessarily have presupposed that the community that was 'blessed' would have to work in order to secure for itself the promised benefits. However the difference of emphasis is striking, and we may legitimately argue that it reflects a further distancing of the wisdom teachers from earlier cultic attitudes. These attitudes are well illustrated by the Book of Deuteronomy, although we should bear in mind that even in this material the oldest concepts of cultic blessing have undergone considerable modification. Deut. 26:1–11 sets out a brief thanksgiving ceremony to accompany the offering of the firstfruits of the harvest. The roots of such a celebration certainly lie, not in the psychological appropriateness of givine 'thanks' to the Divine Giver, but rather in the necessity for returning the first products of the life-giving soil back to the divine source of all 'Life'. Thereby the cycle of life would be kept in motion and the living produce returned to the deity would provide the basis for the continuance of 'life' into the coming season.

A substantial shift in the interpretation of this life-giving 'blessing' is to be found in the extensive series of blessings and cursings set as a concluding section to Deuteronomy (Deut.

28:1–30:20). It is particularly the section dealing with the blessing of the earth in Deut. 28:1–6 which highlights the connections between the divine power mediated through the cult and the fertility and prosperity of the land. The Deuteronomic development has emphasised the idea of obedience to the divine commandments as the determining principle whether Israel is to live under blessing or curse. The roots of this, however, lie in the notion which reaches back into prehistoric times, that blessing, because it was a manifestation of 'life' could only come from a deity and had to be channelled through the cultus.

Against such a background it is not surprising to find that the necessity for work in tilling the earth to produce food could be seen as an unwelcome punishment for all human beings (Gen. 3:17–19). Significantly, in the Babylonian creation story *Enuma Elish*, human beings are viewed as having been created that they might till the earth for the gods. In the Old Testament wisdom teaching a major shift is now seen to be present in the doctrine of work that is presented. In Psalm 104, which displays a number of pronounced wisdom characteristics, it is noteworthy that hard work and the skilful and industrious use of the land and its resources is viewed as part of the wise order of things (cf. Ps. 104:14–23). The opportunity for work, even from early morning until dusk, is looked upon, not as punishment, but as part of a beneficent and providential order. Certainly Ps. 104 has been moulded by the wisdom tradition and it sees no contradiction, or disparity, between the 'free' provision of food and homes for wild animals and birds (Ps. 104:27–28) and the long day's work that human beings must perform. Work is regarded as a good thing, even though the many admonitions rebuking and deploring laziness fully recognize that a deep human tendency to resist the demands of hard work existed. Such, however, was contrary to the teaching of wisdom.

The author of Qoheleth is very well aware that work could be a very strenuous and painful necessity. He recognized the substance of the popular feeling that work seemed to be an unwelcome necessity in a world planned by a divine wisdom. Yet he defends the need for work, by seeing in it a number of benefits, provided that work is not work for its own sake, but work for a greater goal of a secure and happy life (Qoh. 5:12–20).

Perhaps very surprising is the fact that Qoheleth attempts to offer a comprehensive rationale for the nature and necessity of work:

> Then I saw that all toil and all skill in work come from one person's envy of his neighbour.
>
> Qoh. 4:4

Yet work is an obvious necessity since, without it, a person would simply go hungry (Qoh. 4:5). So there are reasons for work, but also reasons why it should not become an obsessive pursuit, which it can do, simply because it has its roots in this envy of one's neighbour (Qoh. 4:6–8). Alongside this Qoheleth points out that much of the pain and misery of work can be softened by the use of a little thought and care:

> If the iron is blunt, and one does not sharpen the edge,
> one must use more strength;
> but wisdom helps one to succeed.
>
> Qoh. 10:10

The message is apparently designed to favour one type of work over another, emphasising the acquisition of skill and the use of the mind, rather than relying on physical strength. What is especially noteworthy is that, although we must presume that the wisdom teachers knew and accepted the cultic idea that the blessing of the earth and the health and vitality of flocks and herds depended upon observance of the rites associated with firstlings and firstfruits, they have interposed a quite new emphasis upon work as the way to success. They do present something that can quite properly be called a work ethic. Work is assumed to be a vital opportunity wherein the individual may succeed, accruing wealth and respect, which his entire household will then benefit from. The path of wisdom is one that is surrounded by many temptations, and among the more alluring of these are the belief that wealth can be acquired quickly, or that hard physical work is not suitable for the truly wise person.

When we put together these varied facets of the way in which wisdom views the household we can see just how emphatically it discloses a shift away from the earlier cultic notions. The household has become the point of central focus. The temple, with its cultus and priesthood, appear only at the fringes of daily life and are treated with respect, but little more. They do not determine the success or failure of the individual family and they do not impinge in any very marked fashion upon the attainment of happiness. Instead the family head is the primary figure whose will and choices determine the destiny of the household which he effectively controls.

Of prime significance too is the economic role which the household has to play. It is regarded as a business venture, for upon its industry and financial health the security of all its members depend. When we look to Qoheleth we find that even the acquisition of considerable riches is looked upon as pointless, if there is no larger family of heirs who can benefit from what has been accrued (Qoh. 4:7–8). The household, and the family which it shelters, represent a key factor in social meaning and success.

We have already pointed out that this emphasis upon the primacy of the household in wisdom is partly to be explained from its popular origins in the oldest levels of folk wisdom. However, the strong emphasis upon the household that predominates in Prov. 1–9 is best seen as expressive of a larger concern than this. It reflects a situation in which Jewish society has been forced back upon its primary institutions, of which the family household is the most fundamental. This well fits our contention that it was in the post-exilic period, when the older clan and tribal structure of early Israel had been broken up, that wisdom presented a new basis for morality, related to the new social pattern of life which had come to prevail.

CHAPTER SIX

Wisdom and the Divine Realm

The question of the extent to which the Israelite–Jewish wisdom tradition displays a distinctive religious character has been answered with a surprising degree of disunity.[1] On the one side there have been scholars who have argued that this tradition of wisdom was so essentially secular and anthropocentric in its character that it cannot properly be looked upon as evidencing a truly religious spirit.[2] Against this can be ranged scholars who have found in wisdom the most thoroughgoing attempt to submit human experience and knowledge of the created order to serious intellectual scrutiny.[3] Since this experience and knowledge drew extensively upon inherited religious beliefs, wisdom itself inevitably assumed a markedly religious character.

---

1. Cf. the significant evaluation of this issue made by Roland E. Murphy, 'Religious Dimensions of Israelite Wisdom', *Ancient Israelite Religion. Essays in Honor of Frank Moore Cross, eds. P. D. Miller, Jr.*, P. D. Hanson, S. Dean McBride, (Philadelphia: Fortress Press, 1987), pp. 449–458.
2. R. E. Murphy, *op. cit.* note 1 above, particularly draws attention to the arguments put forward by H. D. Preuss against conceding any deeply religious character to Israelite wisdom. Cf. H. D. Preuss, 'Alttestamentliche Weisheit in christlicher Theologie?', *BETL* 33 (1974), pp. 165–181; *idem.*, 'Erwägungen zum theologischen Ort alttestamentlicher Weisheitsliteratur', *EvTh.* 30 (1970), pp. 393–417; also 'Das Gottesbild der älteren Weisheit Israels', *Studies in the Religion of Israel*, VTSupp 23 (1923), pp. 117–145.
3. So especially H. H. Schmid, 'Creation as the Broad Horizon', *idem.*, *Wesen und Geschichte der Weisheit*, BZAW 101 (Berlin: A. Töpelmann, 1966); cf. also the pioneering work of H. Gese, *Lehre und Wirklichkeit in der alten Weisheit* (Tübingen: JCBMohr, 1958).

Most scholars would probably find themselves supporting a position somewhere between these two poles in which wisdom occupies a significant place within the many theological currents of the Old Testament, without wishing to claim that it was the most prominent. Probably many would share the view of G. von Rad that for a long period critical approaches to the subject of Old Testament theology underrated the contribution made by wisdom.[4] That wisdom played a notable role can readily be conceded, although what this role actually was has been very variously interpreted.

A point that cannot be overlooked is that wisdom itself did not remain a static and unchanged phenomenon throughout the period during which the Old Testament was taking shape. Not only was there significant literary growth of the wisdom tradition, but its intellectual presuppositions appear to have been subjected to considerable changes. We have, in particular, argued that the place and function of Israelite wisdom changed dramatically from the period before 587 BCE to that which it enjoyed afterwards. The destruction of the state and the rise of the Jewish dispersion were profoundly influential factors in the way in which wisdom developed.

Different models have been adopted to describe the way in which the development of wisdom occurred. A very strongly felt feature has been that of the progressive 'Yahweh-isation', or 'Judaising' of the wisdom tradition, which had originally been part of a fundamentally ancient Near Eastern, and most prominently Egyptian, form of intellectual life. The path towards the integration of wisdom into the Israelite–Jewish world-view was then one of assimilation to more distinctively Israelite ideas of divine revelation and of a divine control of the order of human life which imposed major modifications upon

---

4. Cf. especially G. von Rad, *Wisdom in Israel*, ET J. D. Martin, (London SCM Press, 1982). Von Rad points out that 'Wisdom teaching has often been described as a foreign element in the Old Testament world' (p. 10). We should note also the contribution made by W. Zimmerli in seeking to establish a closer definition of the role played by wisdom in the Israelite religious tradition. Cf. W. Zimmerli, *Old Testament Theology in Outline*, ET David E. Green (Atlanta: John Knox Press, 1978), pp. 155ff.; *Idem, The Old Testament and the World*, ET J. J. Scullion, SJ (London: SPCK, 1976), pp. 43ff.

the older wisdom assumptions.[5] In such a process, it might have been expected that wisdom would have been assimilated to the concepts of covenant and election which enjoy a prominent position in the Pentateuch and Prophets. Yet this clearly did not happen, and it was not until the time of Ben Sira that wisdom and *torah* were drawn into a close alliance. Even here the degree to which a full assimilation has occurred needs to be cautiously estimated. The formal identifications made in Sirach 24 do not wholly correspond to an integrated concept of wisdom-*torah*. Indeed, not until the second and third centuries of the Christian era, with the growth of the Mishnah, is the concept of *torah* worked out in a truly systematised way.

Another model for the development of wisdom that has attained wide and deserved popularity has been one in which a 'crisis' point arose for wisdom within Israelite Jewish history.[6] This may be assumed to have been reached some time after the collapse of the Judean national state. In this tu: strongly pragmatic and anthropocentric character of the earlier wisdom, together with its close political connections, proved unable to accomodate to the realities of Jewish experience. So wisdom was forced to choose between a sterile agnosticism, bordering on cynicism, and an acceptance of the concept of a 'higher wisdom' given by divine revelation.

However, this model too, helpful as it has proved in explaining some of the many-sided characteristics of wisdom, does not cover all aspects of its development. It is arguable that the post-exilic didactic poetry of Proverbs 1–9 represents a genuinely authentic development of the wisdom tradition, whilst displaying a distinctively theologised version of it. In other words its strong theological colouring can be said to belong to intrinsic aspects of the wisdom tradition, without necessarily presupposing that wisdom had undergone a crisis of confidence in its ability to get at the truth.

---

5. Cf. W. McKane, *Proverbs*, p. 10: 'We may conclude that the Instruction which is originally, in Egypt if not in Israel, a means of educating officials, becomes in Israel a method of generalized mundane instruction and thereafter a way of inculcating Yahwistic piety.'

6. Cf. especially J. C. Rylaarsdam, *Revelation in Jewish Wisdom Literature* (Chicago: Univ. of Chicago Press, 1946). We should note also H. Gese, 'Die Krisis der Weisheit bei Kohelet', *Les Sagesses du Proche-Orient ancien* (Paris: Presses Universitaires de France, 1963), pp. 139–151. A number of scholars

The approach adopted here has predominantly been functionalist in its conviction that the use that Israel made of the wisdom tradition after the collapse of the national state was markedly different from that which had earlier prevailed.

The fact that Israel was now a dramatically changed reality in both sociological and political perspectives had a profound impact upon the wisdom tradition. The assumptions of internationalism, the need for a way of life separated from a formal cult centre, the need to define an acceptable moral code based on experience and observation, and for an approach to human problems based on a belief in their inherent solubility by critical observation and insight, all contributed pressures for change. All these requirements were present within the inherited wisdom tradition, formed around the conviction that the world was the product of a skilfully designed and benevolently created order. Wisdom took Judaism into the dispersion and helped to turn the hostile environment of 'unclean lands' into the more acceptable one of a realm of order and design which could be discovered and its rules followed out.

If then we are able to discern features of development, and of a progressive theologising of wisdom, these features have primarily been brought about because wisdom was concerned to co-ordinate and to integrate all aspects of life into one ordered whole. Significantly we have found this process of theologising to have taken place most markedly in areas of thought and activity in which the earlier institutions of the cult and of kingship had dominated. The loss of the 'centre' in the shape of the royal throne and temple of Jerusalem, demanded the provision of a new 'centre' around which intellectual and moral ideas could be clustered. This new 'centre' was found in the notion of wisdom—a wisdom by which the world had been designed and through the operating mechanisms of which life was governed.

---

have believed to find in the writings of Qoheleth and the Book of Job an expression of such a sense of 'crisis', although to do so very much begs the question of the extent to which either of these writings can properly be regarded as originating within the mainstream of the Jewish wisdom tradition.

Accordingly wisdom helped to erode, and ultimately to displace, the fundamentally mythological foundations of the earliest Israelite world-view, the centre of which was in the cult. This was not because wisdom was anti-cultic, but because it was compelled to think and act beyond the borders where the older cultic views of territory, work and social structure prevailed.

Significantly too, in a concern with matters of health and politics, wisdom pressed towards a truly universalist understanding of human needs and obligations. Inevitably therefore wisdom was concerned with all aspects of human relationships and with the defining of a concept of virtue. The fact that it came to do so in terms of a religious commitment—'the fear of the Lord'—is highly significant. It recognised that without this submission to a concept of transcendence—of an other-worldly Reality—the very goundwork of wisdom was defective. Why a person should wish to be wise, rather than a fool, or why it was better to seek happiness and prosperity rather than enjoy the undoubtedly more immediately accessible fruits of wickedness, remained a matter of personal faith and hope. The very foundations of virtue could not readily be viewed from the vantage point of this world and this life alone. Commitment to a truth more absolute than that which could be perceived and affirmed by a lone observer, however shrewd, was necessary.

To this extent we have argued that the consistent trend of biblical wisdom was through and through religious in its thrust. If there was a point of crisis, or more loosely defined, a point at which a *non sequitur* emerged in wisdom's didactic method, it must be found here. Wisdom could observe, and describe with reasonable confidence, the rules of life that corresponded to the order of the world.

That one should adhere to these rules, and believe that this order of the world was ultimately beneficent, required invoking belief in the mind and beneficent purpose of a Creator. The pursuit of wisdom could only be justified by making an appeal to a transcendent authority. The 'beginning', or 'first step', along the path of wisdom had, of necessity, to be found in reverence for the Lord, the Creator and designer of all. To accept that wisdom could provide a trustworthy guide to the problems of living had to be initiated by an initial attitude of reverential fear—this was the indispensable first step of commitment without which the voice of wisdom could not be heard. Such an appeal to the fact of a divine Source and Ground of wisdom meant that it became a truly theological and spiritual feature of Jewish life. It is clothed in this religious garment that it appears before us in the Hebrew Bible.

The Divine Origin of Wisdom

We may take it for granted that the edited collection of proverbial wisdom in the Book of Proverbs has been fully accomodated to a monotheistic faith. The wise insisted that there is but one God and that this deity is known by the name the Lord (Yahweh). If we are to believe the historical picture of the popular religion of pre-exilic Israel that has emerged in recent years, then it would certainly seem that a widespread reverence for other deities alongside, and sometimes in preference to, the Lord was current among many sections of the Israelite population.[7] However the question of one God or many at no point appears to be an issue that has deeply concerned the authors and collectors of our extant Israelite proverbial literature. It may have done so at one time, but, if so, the issue is now wholly submerged beneath the preserved wisdom teaching. In this it is taken for granted that the Lord alone is God.[8]

Since we have followed the view that, during the period of the monarchy, Israel's wisdom sayings were collected and preserved within circles closely linked to the royal court, it is in no way surprising that they now reflect the view of an officially established worship which regarded the Lord alone as God. Yet it is certainly not from the traditional viewpoint of a 'national'

---

7. Cf. now J. S. Holladay, Jr. 'Religion in Israel and Judah under the Monarchy: An Explicitly Archaeological Approach,' *Ancient Israelite Religion. FS Frank Moore Cross, Jr.*, pp. 249–299.

8. The question of the origin and development of monotheism in the Israelite religious tradition is a complex one when set against the wider Near Eastern background. Cf. now Mark S. Smith, *The Early History of God* (San Francisco: Harper & Row, 1990). That wisdom's assumption of a unifying order which prevailed throughout the experienced world assisted in promoting a monotheistic world-view appears highly likely. At the same time a monotheistic religious position fostered the intellectual perspectives adopted by wisdom.

religion that wisdom conceives of the divine realm. The Lord is not merely 'the God of Israel', but quite simply 'God'—the divine Being whose power completely fills the divine realm. As a further outworking of this we find that, no matter how affirmatively wisdom is presented as belonging to the divine side of reality, so that God works in, by and through wisdom, wisdom is in no sense another deity alongside the Lord. Those attempts at tradition–historical analysis which have endeavoured to find in the mediating position of wisdom in Prov. 8:22–23 remnants of an older belief in a goddess of wisdom misread the intention and apologetic character of this important passage. The personified wisdom that appears here is clearly in no sense to be regarded as 'other than', nor even merely 'alongside' the Lord God. Rather she appears as the inalienable bond that unites the creative intention of God with the experienced working of the world. Through wisdom the world can 'know' God and discover the purpose and grandeur of God. She combines within herself aspects of the immanence of deity, coupled with an undeniable transcendence.

In the present context it is important to recognize that proverbial wisdom regularly refers to the divine realm as one controlled and filled by all that was implied in Israel by the use of the divine name.

It comes as no surprise therefore to find that the distinctive name of 'The Lord' is by far the most common title used in Proverbs to refer to the deity. It easily outnumbers the use of the broader, and less nationally distinctive title of God. To a certain degree such a usage marks the most decisive feature of the assimilation of the wisdom tradition to the national religious ethos of Israel. The invocation of the name of the Lord carried with it implications about the nature and intentions of the God who answered to it. Yet the surprising fact is that Israelite wisdom does not attach to the name the familiar qualifications and formal associations that identify this deity as distinctively 'the God of Israel'. Accordingly wisdom teaching shows no interest whatsoever in notions of 'covenant' or of a special 'election' of Israel, either through its royal dynasty, or its central sanctuary. Nor is there any attention given to Israel's occupation of a special 'land', or to its distinctive genealogical origin. The universality of wisdom has

carried with it in the fullest measure the conviction that the
Lord is a universal God. What alone makes Israel a unique
people is the ability to respond in a positive way, through the
fear of the Lord, to the dictates of wisdom which pervade all
creation. Israel's uniqueness is the uniqueness of its wisdom.
We may at this point reflect upon the importance of this
notion for the most positive affirmation of a monotheistic faith
in Judaism. It was of the very essence of the understanding of
wisdom that it was universal in its scope and that its order
prevailed both spatially and temporally throughout the
experienced world. It transcended national barriers, it operated uniformly throughout the seasons, and it did not
anticipate that times would change so as to overturn the
perceived way in which the world is encountered.

To this extent the positing of a supra-natural foundation of
wisdom, and its pre-temporal origin 'before creation', (cf.
Prov. 8:22) serve to reinforce its transcendent divine quality.
Yet it belongs to deity, not alongside, or in any sense apart
from, the Lord as God. It is in this direction that the attempts
to find evidence for a goddess of wisdom[9] in the figure
portrayed metaphorically in Prov. 8:1–23, appear to be of only
limited value, and even to point in the wrong direction. As Isa.
40:13–14. asserts, God did not need an assistant in order to
create and govern the universe.[10] The very Being of God is
'wise' so that all the actions of deity are 'through wisdom'. At
no point can God's action be conceived of as standing outside
of, or apart from, wisdom. All the divine actions embody
wisdom and and so all the created works of God enable this
wisdom of God to be seen and understood by human beings (cf.
Ps. 104:24). To this degree it is the very absence of separate

---

9. Cf. R. N. Whybray, *Wisdom in Proverbs*, Studies in Biblical Theology 45
(London: SCM Press, 1965); idem, 'Proverbs viii 22–31 and its Supposed
Prototypes,' *VT* 15, 1965, pp. 504–514 (reprinted in *Studies in Ancient
Israelite Wisdom*, ed. J. L. Crenshaw (New York: Ktav, 1976) pp. 161–171).
B. Lang, *Frau Weisheit. Deutung einer biblischen Gestalt* (Düsseldorf: Patmos
Verlag, 1975). The cautionary remark of C. V. Camp, *Wisdom and the
Feminine in the Book of Proverbs*, Bible and Literature Series 11 (Sheffield:
Almond Press, 1985), p. 13, is important: 'Personified Wisdom is a literary
figure built up of literary images.'
10. For this important passage cf. the detailed study of R. N. Whybray,
The Heavenly Counsellor in Isaiah xl 13–14, SOTSMS 1 (Cambridge:
Cambridge University Press, 1971).

divine acts, or 'wonders', which makes the reality and power of God recognisable and credible to human beings. The true wonder of creation is found in the orderliness of it all.

The consequences of these fundamental assumptions for the theologizing of wisdom are very considerable and we may argue that its very assumptions favoured a monotheistic interpretation of the divine activity. In fact it is in the theological realm of monotheistic belief that the basic insights of wisdom as a method of understanding and mastering life really come into their own. They work with the assured conviction that a basic harmony binds together the divine providential governance of the world and the perceived connections and consequences of an ordered universe. God's rule is neither arbitrary nor unknowable, even though its ultimate limits are unfathomable, as Job affirms to his friends in Job 12:12–25. To trace the workings of the natural world is to perceive the ordered handiwork of God. In this manner God reveals the divine quality of wisdom through the universe that human beings perceive and which they understand to have been divinely created and fashioned.

Retribution and Morality

The most prominent consequence of this, so far as the theologizing of wisdom is concerned, is to be seen in the way in which the cause and effect relationship which so persistently intrigued and fascinated the early searchers after wisdom is moralised. The principle of retribution dominates the moral teaching of the wise.[11] Bad actions produce bad results and good actions produce good ones. This is not simply an impersonal mechanism that governs life, nor yet a tautology so that what produces bad consequences is bad by self-definition. It is God who has ordained that bad actions, and even actions that are evilly intended, do not go unpunished. So we find that this principle of retribution is asserted as a fixed law of life:

---

11. Cf. G. von Rad, *Wisdom in Israel*, pp. 124ff. K. Koch, 'Is There a Doctrine of Retribution in the Old Testament?' *Theodicy in the Old Testament*, ed. J. L. Crenshaw, Issues in Religion and Theology 4 (London: SPCK, 1983), pp. 57–87 (the original German text appeared in *ZThK* 52, 1955, pp. 1–42).

> The wicked are ruined and are no more,
> but the house of the righteous will stand.
>
> Prov. 12:7

This is effectively the same assertion when God is said to act to bring about such a just ordering of life:

> The Lord is a fortress to the person whose conduct is blameless,[12]
> but destruction to evildoers.
>
> Prov. 10:29

A considerable amount of study has been devoted to this striking preoccupation of the wisdom teachers with the principle of retribution.[13] At times it appears to be thought of as a fixed law that works impersonally, while at others it appeals directly to God as the deity who acts to ensure that actions achieve their proper deserved reward, whether good or bad. In one sense the concept of retribution marks an area where theory and principle seem to take precedence over experienced perceptions of life. In another direction it points to an area where the insistence upon a fixed dogma threatens to generate a certain distance and fixity in the understanding of God. The warm personalism of the descriptions of God as 'Father' to human children—presenting a portrait of One who is 'loving and gracious'—yields place to the image of the Heavenly Schoolmaster, whose eye misses nothing and who has made the rules and expects every one of his creatures to abide by them.

Yet neither of these extremes properly does justice to the origins and intentions of wisdom's concern with a doctrine of retribution as a primary manifestation of the wise ordering of life by God. It is only when such affirmations are made absolute and universal that they begin to reveal their partial and provisional nature. Clearly the teachers of wisdom were sufficiently pragmatic to recognise that the righteous did not always prosper. Awareness of this fact provided for Qoheleth in the third century BCE an important insight to hold up against

---

12. Cf. McKane, *Proverbs*, pp. 226, 427.
13. Besides the works cited above in note 11, cf. W. Zimmerli, *Old Testament Theology in Outline*, p. 159.

the traditional belief in a retributive providence which might be thought to act as a form of natural law (Qoh. 4:1; 7:7; 8:10–13).[14]

Our immediate concern is that this insistence upon the moral governance of the world as an inherent part of the work of divine providence was of fundamental importance to wisdom. It marks the point of most evident and direct assimilation of wisdom's search for order and regularity with the religious belief in God as one who is moral and just and who is present to bless and protect those who put their trust in him. Through the concepts of blessing, righteousness and life the religious vocabulary of piety and worship intersects and overlaps with wisdom's ideas of a natural order which pervades the world and society. Wisdom and piety are not two different, or contrasting, ways of finding harmony and success in life, but are simply two different traditions, or emphases, concerned with experiencing life as God ordained it to be.

It is true that the proponents of wisdom allow that there may be aberrations and distortions to the effectiveness of wisdom in bringing happiness and success. In this case, the truly wise person must not abandon the fundamentals of wisdom, but wait for them to achieve their proper goal. Hence the sapiental sentence instruction can affirm in one of its 'better than . . .' formulations:

> Better is a little in the fear of the Lord
>   than great wealth and trouble with it.[15]
> Prov. 15:16; cf. also Prov. 16:8 and 19:1

It is no surprise therefore to find that the language of piety which asserted God's emotional attitude towards those who revered him could be woven harmoniously into this notion of a principle of retribution at work in the world:

---

14. Cf. J. L. Crenshaw, *Ecclesiastes*, OTL (London: SCM Press, 1989), pp. 101f.; R. N. Whybray, *Ecclesiastes*, NCB (Grand Rapids: W. B. Eerdmans, 1989), 81f., is more questioning whether Qoheleth's attitude in these sayings is intended as criticism of the older wisdom confidence in the experience of retribution in daily life.

15. W. McKane, *Proverbs*, pp. 234, 486f. translates as 'and turmoil with it'. Cf. also R. N. Whybray, *Wealth and Poverty in the Book of Proverbs*, pp. 80, 95 for the manner in which such affirmations reflect wisdom's attitude to the value of wealth.

The conduct of the wicked is an abomination to the Lord,
　　but he loves a person who pursues right action.
                                                    Prov. 15:9

What is especially noteworthy about the presentation of
God's intentions and activity made in the wisdom writings is its
transformation of the idea of a divine 'presence' linked to the
cultus. This has now become totally overlaid by a firm doctrine
of the omnipresence of God:

The eyes of the Lord are everywhere,
　　keeping watch over both bad persons and good.
                                                    Prov. 15:3

Similarly in a different formulation:

Sheol and Abaddon lie open to the Lord
　　how much more the hearts of men.
                                                    Prov. 15:11

The concept of divine presence, so closely linked in the
cultus with notions of 'blessing', is here heavily moralised. God
is the Heavenly Recorder who takes note of all actions
wherever they are performed. Moreover it is not actions alone
that he judges, but the intentions that underlie them. This can
be pressed even more forcibly in a rather Freudian direction to
express the notion that God can perceive, not only the motives
of persons which others do not see, but even the secret
intentions which we hide from ourselves:

All the actions of a person are blameless in his own opinion,
　　but the Lord weighs the intention.[16]
                                                    Prov. 16:2

Every action of a person is right in his own opinion,
　　but the Lord considers the motives.[17]
                                            Prov. 21:2; cf. also 17:3

---

16. The word translated here as 'intention' is literally 'spirit' (Heb. *ruah*),
which several times denotes the initiating force of human action.
17. Although very close to the formulation of Prov. 16:2 the statement here
has 'heart' (= mind, intention, motive).

The veil of self-justification which we draw over our intentions can never hide them from God.

Wisdom and Worship

The strong emphasis upon self-examination and a genuine searching of the individual heart indicates how profoundly the theologizing of wisdom has led to an intensified moralising of the language of worship. As we have already noted in the manner in which the idea of the fear of the Lord has overtaken that of blessing achieved through the rituals of sacrifice, so cultic language generally appears to have been strongly moralised by the proponents of wisdom. Nowhere is this more strikingly seen than in the assertion:

The sacrifice of a wicked person is an abomination;
and even more so when it is offered with a bad conscience.[18]

Prov. 21:27

This cannot be dismissed as displaying an attitude of simple neutrality towards the cultus. It goes deeper than this, not overtly rejecting the sacrifices of the wicked in the way the prophets had done (cf. Isa. 1:10–11; Jer. 7:21–26; Amos. 5:21–24), but moralising the belief in their efficacy. Consequently wickedness comes to be defined quite precisely in a manner that places the greatest weight upon bad intentions and designs.

It is particularly noteworthy that the concept of 'abomination' (Heb. *to'ebhah*), which appears primarily to have been used in the context of worship and to have connoted a quasi-physical sense of taboo, is a favoured term in wisdom. It is used very broadly to describe a wide range of reprehensible actions. At times it retains the central core of its earlier close connections with the cult. In this it indicated actions and objects which are repudiated by God. In wisdom, however, it has taken on a much broader range of meaning as an abstract noun, defining activities that are bad. By describing certain

---

18. NRSV has the more familiar 'with evil intent', but the sense appears to be of a worshipper acting with the awareness that what he, or she, is doing is out of harmony with other actions.

lines of conduct as an 'abomination' the wisdom teachers affirmed that the actions so defined were reprehensible in society as a whole. If any narrowly religious connotation remains in the noun it is in asserting that the type of conduct that constitutes an 'abomination' is one which contravenes the demands of the fear of the Lord.

This preference in vocabulary usage appears to have been a deliberate attempt to extend into a wider moral sphere a fundamental concept, originally based on notions of uncleanness and taboo, that had a special currency in the language of worship. It shows how the theologizing of wisdom achieved a very forceful combination of ideas which affirmed that a moral order prevailed within the social realm. This order related concepts of providence and divine governance with notions of a divine presence in worship. The wisdom teachers have at no point abandoned the belief that fundamentally it is the wise ordering of life in accordance with God's will that constitutes the moral order of the world.

This is carried in a direction which suggests that the best contribution that worship can make to the wellbeing of human beings is to symbolize and remind the worshipper of the right moral attitude that is needful for a happy and long life. When this is achieved then the activities of worship in procuring the forgiveness of sin through atonement become needless:

> By loyalty and faithfulness wrongdoing is covered,
> and a person avoids evil by the fear of the Lord.
>   Prov. 16:6

We have already pointed out that this belief in a rather abstract moral order in the world appears ultimately to have led to a certain deistic tendency in the wisdom teaching. In this God lies hidden in, and to some extent bound by, the rules of order, justice and morality which permeate all life and extend throughout the world. The most striking example of this deistic tendency is to be seen in Qoheleth. In urging a reverent and committed attitude towards God in worship, and in the respecting the making of vows and votive offerings, the author presses the necessity for a very strict discipline (Qoh. 5:1-7). In doing so he expresses the frequently quoted words 'for God is in heaven, while you are upon earth, therefore let your words be few' (Qoh. 5:2). The image that this conjures up is of God as a rather distant, but very careful record keeper, the Heavenly Tally-man!

A further implication of this conviction is that, for the time being, God will leave the rules permitting human freedom to operate, but in the end he will make up a final account which will have to be paid (cf. Qoh. 8:12–13). The 'rules' appear to have become so important that the divine Ruler is almost hidden behind them. Consequently much of the sense of personal warmth and caring which Israel expressed through its powerful use of metaphors of fatherhood and motherhood in its portrayal of God have fallen into the background.

It would be possible to argue that wisdom has so emphasised the note of divine transcendence that the sense of divine immanence in the world has been relegated to a minor role. Yet this is hardly true overall, for not only do we have the important affirmation concerning the mediating role of wisdom in Prov. 8:22–31, but the presence of this wise order operating in the world is taken to be evidence of the divine reality. Providence is ordered and just, and comprehends both the physical universe as well as the relationships of individuals to each other. Nevertheless it is truly a divine providence and its loving and beneficent goal for all human beings is repeatedly stressed. The operation of wisdom in the world is viewed as the day to day manifestation of a divine providence.

What is impressive is the way in which wisdom insists that there are no short-cuts for individuals which could lead to a favoured or special relationship to God for a few.

A feature that is very noteworthy in wisdom's doctrine of the divine providential order for humankind is to be seen in the importance which it attaches to prayer. If the rites and activities of the cultus show little appeal for the wise, and are largely left to operate under the priestly oversight without overt criticism, yet the very heart of any human relationship to God is found by them in personal prayer.

> The sacrifice of the wicked is an abomination to the Lord
> but the prayer of an upright person is his delight.
>
> Prov. 15:8

The Lord is far from the wicked,
  but he hears the prayer of right-acting persons.
                                    Prov. 15:29

This insistence that prayer can only be effective if it is the expression of a life that accords with the demands of righteous living is found repeated again:

If a person turns away his ear from hearing instruction,
even his prayer becomes an abomination.
                                    Prov. 28:9

In this the idea of 'instruction' (Heb. *torah*) can best be understood to refer to wisdom teaching in a broad sense, rather than as a reference to the written *torah*. Not until a very late period does the term appear to refer in wisdom sayings to the written scripture.[19]

It is not difficult for us to see that certain genuine tensions exist in the picture of providence that the wise have advocated, yet it is necessary to recognize that we have ourselves not found it easy to reconcile such conflicting insights with each other. On the one hand the world is portrayed as a fixed, and relatively self-contained, system of principles and ordered laws. Human beings must conform to these and work within them for they are indeed 'laws of life'. Against this, however, the personal nature of God and the possibility of direct divine intervention to uphold what is right and overthrow what is evil, are fully maintained. So there is still some room in the teaching of wisdom for 'personal providences' and for the individual to seek out God and to maintain a personal relationship with him. Overall, however, the major emphasis is that divine providence is chiefly to be discerned in the consistency and universality of the operation of wisdom in the world. The way of wisdom is the will of God for individuals and for the entire human race.

Nevertheless, when we turn to the more guarded statements of Qoheleth, we find that this concept of a personal relationship between God and human individuals acquires a rather weak

---

19. Cf. my essay, 'Wisdom', *It is Written. Scripture Citing Scripture. Essays in Honour of Barnabas Lindars*, eds. D. A. Carson and H. G. M. Williamson (Cambridge: CUP, 1988), pp. 67–83.

and pallid complexion. Over against the inherited doctrine of God's wise and righteous rule Qoheleth draws attention to the fact that often divine retribution appears not to be evident in human affairs (Qoh. 8:4). The best that can be done to defend the concept is to leave it to an unknown afterlife (Qoh. 8:12–13). So the truly wise person will have to come to terms with the experience that the wicked are often able to 'get away with it' during their lifetime. Qoheleth even goes so far as to point out that such flouting of the sense of a just order may follow the wicked to the grave for even then hypocritical eulogies may be be uttered (Qoh. 8:10–11). Such is the freedom and propensity of human society to oppose the dictates of wisdom that even at the funeral of the wicked the words of condemnation which such a person has merited are never expressed.

Divine Sovereignty and Human Responsibility

This awareness of a divine overruling providence that controls all human activities has certainly left the teachers of wisdom with some dilemmas which border on the point of paradox. If God is the ultimate Ruler and Master of Life, and has established the principles of wisdom which govern all human actions, then what place is left for prayer and a personal relationship with him? The answer to this question appears to have been sought by the wise in recognizing that a mysterious limit existed to how much human beings could discern the full extent of the working of divine providence. So humility before the mystery of God's will and a sincere trusting in a gracious divine purpose remained important for the truly wise person. Some things could never be known in advance, nor the outcome of all actions foreseen:

> With his mind a person plans his way,
>   but the Lord directs his steps.
> Prov. 16:9

Rather unexpectedly we find the assertion that individual human beings may not be fully responsible for the consequences of what they say. They may speak before they have truly thought through what they are saying; they may be misunderstood, or their words may provoke a response which they did not intend:

> The plans of the mind belong to a person,
>> but the answer of the tongue is from the Lord.
>>> Prov. 16:1

The meaning here would appear to be that right speaking and verbal expression is so important that a person cannot be in full control of it. Only by trusting one's speech to God to convey the intended message can the proper result be achieved. Or is the purpose of the instruction to urge great caution in speech by alerting the pupil to the dangers of expressing himself, or herself, so badly as to misrepresent the intended message. At any rate the overall effect is to insist that we are judged by what we actually say, not by what we intended to say. Therefore due caution and an openness to what God requires, are in order.

The same principle can be said to apply to all human plans and actions:

> With the mind a person thinks up many plans,
>> but it is the purpose of the Lord that will be carried out.
>>> Prov. 19:21

We can certainly recognize here parallels with familiar aphorisms of our own. Such a recognition that even the wisest of human beings cannot be in full mastery of life is used to urge a proper humility in the face of life's demands and difficulties. Human frailty and ignorance generate an awareness of the need to search out wisdom diligently:

> A man's steps are ordered by the Lord;
>> how then can man understand his way?
>>> Prov. 20:24

The aim here is surely not to express despair about using thought and reason to plan one's life adequately, but rather the opposite. Even the greatest care and the most comprehensive plans can never be enough to master the risks and problems that face each individual. A proper attitude of humility and submission to God's will is therefore necessary. This humility is no excuse for a failure to use reasonable thought, but it denotes a proper awareness that the complexities of life are such that they will exceed the competence of human understanding. Even more is this principle, which governs the sense of a divine providence controlling individual lives, operative on the larger scale of human history:

> The horse is made ready for the day of battle,
> but the victory belongs to the Lord.
>
> Prov. 21:31

We can sense here that the proponents of wisdom have inherited traditions which do not harmonize readily with each other. On the one hand the very understanding of God implies concepts of divine sovereignty and power. It is the divine will that must prevail. Alongside this, however, there stands the conviction of the wise that it is the very goal of seeking wisdom that one should be in a position to master life. If there is order in the world, then this order can be observed and understood so that life can be lived in an enriching and successful way. The working of divine providence, which is the way of wisdom, can be observed in the world. However this way cannot be so completely discerned and acted upon that all element of mystery is removed. Consequently the need for submission to God and for trust in him remains paramount.

This conviction regarding the ultimate inscrutability of the divine will appears to motivate the sentence instruction concerning the seeking of oracular signs through the sacred lot. This has important repercussions for understanding the attitude of the wise towards a prominent aspect of organised worship:

> The lot is cast into the lap,
> but the decision is wholly from the Lord.
>
> Prov. 16:33

On the face of it this would appear to be expressing a truth that was taken for granted in the cultic sphere. The sacred lot, which is primarily known in the form of the Urim and Thummim (cf. Exod. 28:30.), was a means of discovering the

divine will. It was used in military operations (cf. 2 Sam. 2:1;
5:19, 23, 25), and probably also in cases where recovery from
illness was in question (cf. Hezekiah's consultation with the
prophet Isaiah, Isa. 38:1–8). Primarily, however, it was used as
a means of resolving otherwise insoluble legal disputes (cf.
Deut. 17:8–13).

We can see, both from the legal provisions of the Old
Testament and from the eventual discontuance of the use of the
sacred lot, that its use was not regarded as very satisfactory.
The saying of Prov. 16:33 therefore can hardly be intended as
an affirmation of the suitability of the sacred lot as a means of
knowing the divine will. Rather it seems to imply that such a
simple mechanistic attempt to discover the will of God can
never properly uncover so majestic and inscrutable a reality. Its
intention therefore would appear to be to urge caution and
doubt about such a cultic institution on the grounds that the
divine will was too profound a reality to be discovered so easily.
If this is so then it fits smoothly along with the sayings which
insist even the most diligent searching can never find out the
whole will of God.

The Importance of the Inner Life

An especially interesting feature of the teaching of wisdom lies
in the extent to which it explores the inner life of human
beings. If the divine origin of the universe and the providential
governance of its history are to be seen in the wisdom that
pervades all things, then the appropriation of this wisdom must
be a divine activity. So, since the search for wisdom is an
activity of the mind, then it is in the mind of human beings that
God is most directly active. He is at work in human thinking
and planning and, through the constant need for such activity,
the individual person is brought into an encounter with the
divine. So prayer is the highest of all religious activities because
it is an encounter between the individual and the Sovereign of
the universe:

> Commit your work to the Lord,
>   and your plans will be established.
>   Prov. 16:3

In line with the recognition that a close bond exists between thought and speech we find the sentence instruction:

> The plans of the wicked are an abomination to the Lord,
> but gracious words are pure.[20]
>
> Prov. 15:26

The sapiental instruction paid great attention to the fact that the roots of action lay in the thoughts and intentions of the mind. Only the fool allowed himelf to be drawn into unpremeditated acts. Often these thoughts and plans remained inscrutable and could only be discovered by a person's actions, or by the experienced perceptiveness of the truly wise man:

> The purpose in a man's mind is like deep water,
> but a man of discernment will draw it out.
>
> Prov. 20:5

It is very hard for us to define with any precision the exact categories of mental activity that governed this inner world of thought and intention. It would be all too easy to describe it as a process of reasoning, since reasoning certainly enters into what is described. Yet it is not reason alone, in the Greek sense, that is being referred to, since there is no separate category of rational logic that can define what is reasonable. Rather it is a combination of experience, innate caution and even a measure of distrust that enables the wise man to show understanding. If even the wisest of persons cannot discern all that motivates the human spirit, and if we are prone even to deceive ourselves about our actions, then only God can see into the deepest recesses of the mind.

This seems to be the implication of the assurance:

> The spirit of man is the lamp of the Lord,
> searching all his most inward being.[21]
>
> Prov. 20:27

---

20. W. McKane, *Proverbs*, pp. 234, 483 defines such 'gracious words' as 'words of goodwill spoken with benevolent intent'.

21. The thought which underlies the verse is remarkably profound, and yet is wholly characteristic of wisdom's interest in the inner life. McKane, p. 547 defines the saying as 'a confident assertion that he (the mere human being)

One phrase that appears to have been a distinct coining of the wise of ancient Israel has been passed on to us as one of the most distinctive descriptions of the truly Christian ethic. This is the 'purity of heart' which is found in the difficult saying of Prov. 22:11:

> The person who loves purity of heart,
>   and whose speech is gracious,
>   will have the king as his friend.[22]

As a sacrifice offered in the cultus had to be pure; that is unblemished and free from disease, so should the wise person strive to attain a completely unblemished attitude of mind. This called for a degree of integrity of purpose and innocence of intention that made right speaking and right action the natural thing to do. This could not be achieved unless the deceptiveness of human motives and the persistence of bad feelings and attitudes was fully recognized:

> Who can say, 'I have made my heart clean;
>   I am pure from my sin'?
>
> Prov. 20:9

So, when adopted into the early Christian community, the attainment of purity of heart could be presented as that Christian virtue which made the vision of God possible:

> Blessed are the pure in heart,
>   for they shall see God.
>
> Matt. 5:8

Overall it is impressive to realize how extensively the inwardness of piety and moral teaching that characterises the teaching of Jesus in the Gospels has drawn upon the insights that were established by the wisdom tradition of ancient Israel.

---

need not be a victim of self-deceit since he has this inner light on which he can rely. He has the power of introspection by which he can examine the depths of his self and see clearly in Yahweh's light what is there.'
22. The translation of the text is far from clear; cf. McKane, *Proverbs*, pp. 567ff. who renders very differently.

If the claims of Burton L. Mack[23] that Jesus should primarily be interpreted as a Jewish teacher of wisdom may be criticised as rather one-sided, nevertheless it represents an important corrective to the fashionable portrait of a generation ago. In this the notion of Jesus as a radical apocalyptic visionary and religious reformer paid far too little heed to the Jewish wisdom inheritance in the ethical and spiritual teaching of the Gospels.

Wisdom and Mantic Power

There is a further important area concerned with the pursuit of wisdom which needs to be examined with very considerable care. If wisdom is the key to attaining success and security in life, and the Lord, the God of Israel, is recognized to be the creative source and providential upholder of wisdom, then may there not be some secret and uniquely efficacious way of obtaining this wisdom? May there not in fact be another esoteric tradition of wisdom, unknown to the majority of mankind, but known to a few initiates? This is an assumption that underlies a great deal of teaching concerning magic and mantic practices. It lived on in European thought in an influential way into the late Middle Ages under the guise of 'the powerful philosophy'.[24] Certainly we find in the Old Testament, alongside the formal and established tradition of wisdom that is preserved in Proverbs and Ecclesiastes, references to a type of wisdom expertise that appears to have been very different.

The foremost instances of such a tradition are to be seen in the Joseph story and in the traditions concerning Daniel. Joseph's ability as an interpreter of dreams (Gen. 40:1–41:36) is taken as illustrative of the fact that he was a man who was 'wise and discreet' (Gen. 41:39). Similarly, in the later book of Daniel, Daniel's ability to interpret dreams is ascribed to his possession of a wisdom superior to that of the wise men of Babylon (Dan. 2:12–30). Belief that there did exist such a

---

23. Burton L. Mack, *A Myth of Innocence. Mark and Christian Origins* (Philadelphia: Fortress Press, 1988).
24. Cf. Frances A. Yates, *The Occult Philosophy in the Elizabethan Age* (London: Routledge and Kegan Paul, 1979). Cf. also Howard Clark Kee, *Medicine, Miracle and Magic in New Testament Times*, SNTSMS 55 (New York: CUP, 1986), pp. 95ff.

special and esoteric branch of wisdom which remained apart from, and superior to, other more widely known wisdom instruction has clearly influenced the language of St. Paul in 1 Cor. 2:6–13. Yet the apostle here turns such teaching on its head since it is not a secret and hidden wisdom that outclasses the wisdom of the world but the divine action in redemption through the Cross of Christ.

Much discussion has been devoted to the question of the extent to which the collection of stories concerning the patriarch Joseph can properly be said to have been influenced by Israelite wisdom.[25] Similarly further questions hover around the ascription of the epithet 'wise' to the figure of Daniel and the degree to which the mainsteam tradition of wisdom has affected the rise of the apocalyptic writing of the book of Daniel.[26] Clearly we are faced here with a very different kind of wisdom from that found either in Proverbs or Qoheleth. Yet it is certainly possible that some element of overlap existed between what we may describe as this tradition of mantic wisdom and the more central tradition of wisdom instruction.

It is highly probable that the idea of a special wisdom which included knowledge of magic crafts and secrets was at one time a part of the popular folk life of ancient Judaism. Undoubtedly there are features present in this mantic wisdom, and the folk motifs which abound in stories referring to it, which suggest that it once formed part of a quite widespread and popular part of Jewish life. Indeed it may be argued that it represents a feature of daily life and popular folklore that have powerfully affected the lives of people across large areas of the civilised

---

25. A very affirmative position was advocated by G. von Rad, 'Josephsgeschichte und altere Chokma', *VTSupp 1, Strasbourg Congress Volume* (1953), pp. 120–127 (= *Gesammelte Studien zum Alten Testament* ThB 8 (Munich: Chr. Kaiser, 1958, pp. 272–280). More critical positions are advocated by J. L. Crenshaw, 'Method in Determining Wisdom Influence upon "Historical" Literature', *JBL* 88 (1969), pp. 129–142; G. W. Coats, 'The Joseph Story and Ancient Wisdom: A Reappraisal', *CBQ* 35 (1973), pp. 285–297; *ibid. From Canaan to Egypt: Structural and Theological Context for the Joseph Story*, CBQMS 4 (1976); C. Westermann, *Genesis 37–50*, ET J. J. Scullion SJ (London: SPCK, 1986), pp. 26f.

26. Cf. the discussion in E. W. Nicholson, 'Apocalyptic', *Tradition and Interpretation*, ed. G. W. Anderson (Oxford: OUP, 1979), pp. 189–213, esp. pp. 207ff.; P. D. Hanson, 'Apocalyptic Literature', *The Hebrew Bible and its Modern Interpreters*, eds. D. A. Knight and G. M. Tucker (Philadelphia: Fortress/Decatur: Scholars Press, 1985) pp. 465–488.

world to the present day. Where literacy and learning become avenues to power and prosperity, it seems almost inevitable that there should appear to exist secret codes and formulae which make possible a fast lane to such goals.

However, nothing in the Old Testament or the New can substantiate the claim that such a tradition of mantic wisdom formed anything other than a bizarre sub-culture of Jewish life. It remained an offshoot and an aberration from the primary goals of wisdom. These depended on openness to critical investigation, a strong insistence that right thinking and right living formed the foundations of the good life, and a conviction that the paths of wisdom that led to life had been recognizable for all to see since the foundation of the world. Over against such there could be no secret wisdom which would have meant that God disowned his impartiality in making the truths of wisdom potentially available to all. The whole trend of the preserved tradition of wisdom represented in the books of Proverbs, Qoheleth and Ben Sira is strongly and effectively against belief in the efficacy of a secret mantic wisdom. Perhaps we must recognise that, where a strong religious tradition marches ahead in a particular direction, it is almost inevitable that it should spawn a distinctive sub-culture in which many of its primary goals and restraints are disregarded.

The subject of mantic wisdom, however, raises the important question of the attitude of Jewish wisdom to magic and its distinctive assumptions.[27] A very major point arose as an outworking of the conviction that, in a monotheistic religious environment, there could be no stream of wisdom which lay outside the gracious and just providence of God. Wisdom derived from him alone and so there could be no wisdom that conflicted with his divine will:[28]

No wisdom, no intelligence, no plan,
  can prevail against the Lord
                        Prov. 21:30

---

27. Howard Clark Kee, *op. cit.*, pp. 112ff.
28. Cf. J. Fichtner, 'Die Bewältigung heidnischer Vorstellungen und Praktiken in der Welt des Alten Testaments', *Gottes Weisheit*, AzT II/3, ed. K. D. Fricke (Stuttgart: Calwer Verlag, 1965), pp. 115–129.

We have also noted earlier that it appears to have been a quite favoured technique of the wise to employ such images as those of 'the tree of life' and the 'fountain of life' simply as metaphors in praise of wisdom. Clearly it mattered greatly to the teachers of wisdom to demonstrate that there was nothing mysterious or mythical about the obtaining and application of wisdom. What hindered most people from benefiting from wisdom was their own wilful obstinacy in refusing its guidance.

In a similiar vein we discover, almost incidentally, that ancient Israel was fully familiar with belief in the power of magical objects such as stones, since they can be referred to in a metaphorical sense (Prov. 17:8). It is also highly probable that Qoheleth's sharp rebuttal of the belief that it was possible to discover what lay hidden in the future (Qoh. 3:21; 6:12; 8:17) reflects familiarity with popular claims regarding the unique oracular endowments of special persons and objects. Certainly therefore it is evident that the preserved wisdom of the Old Testament has not simply omitted to include examples of a type of mantic wisdom but has consciously rejected it.

It is not difficult to see how the superimposing of a carefully worked through tradition of wisdom upon a society that had been traditionally strongly moulded by a priestly tradition of cultus should have created problems. The belief in miracles which lay outside the wise order of a divinely governed world had a powerful hold upon the popular mind and a firm place in the Israelite tradition. Similarly priestly ideas of 'life' and 'blessing', and the harmful power of a solemn curse, all suggested that various forms of special power existed in the world. Overall, however, the teachers of wisdom appear to have held fast to their conviction that order prevailed in the world and that God was best seen and known in and through this order, not outside it.

So it may be argued that wisdom contributed strongly to the decline of popular folklorist types of magic in ancient Judaism. God was not a God of secret powers and closely guarded mysteries. His wisdom lay open for all to see in the life of the world and the upholding of a just and beneficial structure to society. What hindered the appropriation of this wisdom and the moulding of all human life in accordance with its dictates was the perversity of the nature of evil and the wilful refusal of wrongdoers to listen to the wise teaching given to them. If there was mystery left in the universe it was the mystery of iniquity and the strange obstinacy of the fool who showed himself to be impervious to the wealth of good teaching which was available, but which he, or she, stubbornly refused to hear.

Wisdom and Divine Revelation

Since the valuable and instructive work of J. C. Rylaarsdam, the question of the way in which wisdom has understood and presented the nature of divine revelation has received considerable, and well merited, attention.[29] To a significant degree the further researches of H. Gese and H. H. Schmid in drawing attention to the manner in which wisdom builds upon convictions concerning the order and regularity that is evident in the world have strengthened this conviction.[30] Wisdom appears strongly, at least in its developing stages, to have favoured the belief in what we should describe as 'natural revelation'. God is known in and through the works that he has made. Creation itself is the handiwork of a divine wisdom, as Prov. 8:22 affirms. That there should stand alongside this a quite separate realm of truth, known only to a few to whom it has been uniquely disclosed, would seem to belong outside the more fundamental convictions of wisdom, if not actually to contradict them.

Yet in fact, through the oracle-giving techniques of worship and through the inspired words of prophets, such beliefs appear to have survived side by side in ancient Israel without any obvious degree of conflict. Only in the course of time, and more obviously through the pressures generated by a need for a coherent and co-ordinated body of canonical *torah*, did the conflicts and incongruities of the two types of revelation manifest themselves. It is the awareness of this fact that has generated the belief among scholars that Jewish wisdom experienced a period of 'crisis' in which the inadequacies of the

---

29. J. C. Rylaarsdam, *Revelation in Jewish Wisdom Literature, passim.*
30. See above p. 151 note 3.

older wisdom belief in a purely natural revelation of God showed themselves.[31]

However the difficulty has been to demonstrate how, and when, such a crisis may have arisen and how significantly it differed from the other clashes and contradictions that had to be smoothed out before the Old Testament could emerge. In fact it may be argued that the very emergence of post-exilic Judaism is itself essentially one prolonged response to a crisis. This was fundamentally the crisis of the break-up of the remnants of the Judean state in 587 BCE and the destruction of the Jerusalem temple. At one single blow the old order of political and intellectual life was demolished and a new order had to be introduced. A whole range of compromises and re-evaluations had to take place before the restoration of an effective religious life became possible. This came increasingly to be centred upon a concept of a written *torah* and the progressive extension of this throughout Jewish life.

Before long the necessity for correct interpretation of this *torah* became itself a major religious undertaking, giving rise to a new class of religious leadership. In all of this wisdom played a role and, of necessity, the contents of this wisdom had to be brought into line with the dictates of the central body of *torah*.[32] All of this has been usefully noted and documented, so that the crisis it brought for wisdom was not especially unique to the wisdom tradition. As the importance of the concept of revelation through a written *torah* became more central to Jewish life, so inevitably were the teachings of wisdom subordinated to the more fundamental emphases of the written law. This point is made in a rather prosaic and self-assured manner by the editor who has added in Qoh. 12:13–14 a concluding admonitory note to the more adventurous thoughts of this writer.

In one area, however, the character and insights of Israelite–Jewish wisdom do have a significant contribution to make to the understanding of divine revelation in the Old Testament.

---

31. See above p. 153 note 6.
32. Cf. G. T. Sheppard, *Wisdom as a Hermeneutical Construct*, BZAW 151 (Berlin and New York: W. de Gruyter, 1980) and my essay 'Wisdom', (note 19 above), pp. 75ff.

This concerns the extent to which the characteristic emphasis upon the role of great charismatic individuals has been modified within the wisdom tradition. In a very remarkable fashion the claim that Israel's life and religion were shaped by great charismatic leaders pervades a large area of the Old Testament literature. Whether through the prominence given to the person of Moses, to the roles of Saul and David in founding Israel's monarchy, or through the prophets, the central body of the Old Testament literature establishes its authority as revealed truth by appeal to the great leaders through whom it was mediated. The concept of revelation is inseparably linked to the belief that certain individuals were endowed with unique insight and gifts of leadership.

To some degree it could be argued that the claim to Solomonic authorship of several of the wisdom writings follows along the same path. Nevertheless the figure of Solomon is not essential to wisdom in the way that Moses is to the *torah*, or David to the kingship, nor even the prophets to the books of prophecy. Nor is it surprising that wisdom came to interpret the significance of the great figures of Israel's past in very new directions in an effort to render them suitable as examples of wisdom. This has served to broaden very considerably the emphasis upon the understanding of divine revelation as mediated through uniquely charismatic individuals. Such individuals are regarded as examples and types whom others can follow, rather than as incomparable figures of an unrepeatable past. In its understanding of the way in which God reveals his will through human beings, wisdom has given a warmer and more easily recognisable interpretation of the human situation.

Selected Bibliography

The following books are especially recommended for further reading on the subject of Israelite and Jewish wisdom literature. Those marked with * contain extensive bibliographies of recent studies in the subject:

J. L. Crenshaw, *Old Testament Wisdom, An Introduction* (London: SCM Press, 1982).*

——(ed.), *Studies in Ancient Israelite Wisdom* (New York: Ktav, 1976).

——(ed.), *Theodicy in the Old Testament*, Issues in Religion and Theology 4, (London: SPCK, 1984).

——(ed. with J. T. Willis), *Essays in Old Testament Ethics* (New York: Ktav, 1974).

——*Ecclesiastes. A Commentary*, OTL (London: SCM Press, 1989).

——'The Wisdom Literature', *The Hebrew Bible and Its Modern Interpreters*, ed. D. A. Knight and G. M. Tucker (Philadelphia: Fortress Press/Decatur: Scholars Press, 1985), pp. 369–407.*

J. A. Emerton, 'Wisdom Literature', *Tradition and Interpretation*, ed. G. W. Anderson (Oxford: Oxford University Press, 1979), pp. 214–237.*

M. V. Fox *Qoheleth and His Contradictions*, JSOTSupp 71 (Sheffield: Sheffield Academic Press, 1989).

J. G. Gammie & L. Perdue, *The Sage in Israel and the Ancient Near East* (Winona Lake: Eisenbrauns, 1990).*

W. McKane, *Prophets and Wise Men*, SBT 44 (London: SCM Press, 1965).

——*Proverbs. A New Approach*, OTL, (London: SCM Press, 1975).

B. L. Mack and R. E. Murphy, 'Wisdom Literature', *Early Judaism and Its Modern Interpreters*, ed. R. A. Kraft and G. W. E. Nickelsburg (Philadelphia: Fortress Press/Scholars Press: Atlanta, 1985), pp. 371–410.*

D. F. Morgan, *Wisdom in the Old Testament Traditions*, (Atlanta: John Knox Press, 1981).

——*Between Text and Community. The 'Writings in Canonical Interpretation*, (Minneapolis: Augsburg Fortress, 1990).

R. E. Murphy, *Wisdom Literature. Job, Proverbs, Ruth, Canticles, Ecclesiastes, Esther* (Grand Rapids: Wm.B. Eerdmans, 1981).

——'Religious Dimensions of Israelite Wisdom', *Ancient Israelite Religion. FS F. M. Cross, Jr.*, ed. P. D. Miller, Jr., P. D. Hanson & S. D. McBride (Philadelphia: Fortress Press, 1987), pp. 449–458.

G. Ogden, *Qoheleth*, (Sheffield: JSOT Press, 1987).

G. von Rad, *Wisdom in Israel*, ET James D. Martin (London: SCM Press, 1972).

R. B. Y. Scott, *The Way of Wisdom in the Old Testament*, (New York: Macmillan, 1971).

R. N. Whybray, *Wisdom in Proverbs*, SBT 45, (London: SCM Press, 1965).

——*The Intellectual Tradition in the Old Testament*, BZAW 135 (Berlin—New York: W. de Gruyter, 1974).

——*Ecclesiastes*, NCB (Grand Rapids: Wm. B. Eerdmans, 1989)

——*Ecclesiastes*, Old Testament Guides (Sheffield: Sheffield Academic Press, 1989).

——*Wealth and Poverty in the Book of Proverbs*, JSOTSupp 99 (Sheffield: Sheffield Academic Press, 1990).

Author index

Ackroyd, P.R. 30, 57, 97, 113
Alt, A. 19

Bailey, L.R.Sr. 72
Barth, C.F. 74
Becker, J. 60, 62, 114
Benjamin, Dom C. 110
Brueggemann, W. 104, 107
Bryce, G.E. 21, 40
Burchardt, C. 133

Camp, C.V. 140f., 142f., 158
Causse, A. 29f.
Childs, B.S. 14f., 21
Clements, R.E. 18, 52, 104, 112, 114, 166
Clifford, R.J. 52
Coats, G.W. 173
Cohn, R.L. 52, 54
Collins, J.J. 15
Crenshaw, J.L. 14, 21, 41f., 50, 90, 104, 107, 118, 129, 161, 173

Day, J. 54
Derousseaux, L. 60
Deurloo, K.A. 105
Doll, P. 135
Douglas, M. 56f., 66, 76
Driver, G.R. 67, 101

Eichrodt, W. 13, 20
Emerton, J.A. 14

Fichtner, J. 19, 132f., 175
Field, M. 75

Fox, M.V. 50
Frick, F.S. 110
Fuhs, H.F. 60

Gammie, J.G. 59
Gerleman, G. 99
Gerstenberger, E. 60, 137
Gese, H. 17, 19, 151, 153, 177
Good, E.M. 84
Gordis, R. 125
Gorman, F.H., Jr. 48, 72

Hanson, P.D. 97, 113, 123, 174
Haran, M. 107
Harrelson, W.L. 54
Hasel, G.F. 13, 69
Haspecker, J. 60
Heaton, E.W. 19
Hengel, M. 16, 90
Hill, C. 126, 130
Holladay, J.S. Jr. 156

Johnson, A.R. 69

Kaiser, O. 55f.
Kayatz, C. 24
Kee, H.C. 66, 173, 175
Kellermann, D. 133
Klein, R.W. 58
Klopfenstein, M.A. 37
Koch, K. 159
Knibb, M.A. 69
Kraus, H.-J. 48, 53
Kreuzer, S. 72f.
Kühlewein, J. 133

Kuntz, J.K. 17

di Lella, A.A. 92
Lichtheim, M. 95

McCarthy, D.J. 97
McKane, W. 59, 79f., 98ff., 131,
   134ff., 146, 153, 160f., 171f.
Mack, B.L. 14ff., 173
Marbock, J. 92f.
Martens, E.A. 13
Mendenhall, G.E. 127
Meyers, E.M. 25
Miles, J.C. 67
Morgan, D.F. 17
Mowinckel, S. 16, 114
Mueller, U.B. 73
Müller, H.-P. 40, 59
Murphy, R.E. 14, 151

Nicholson. E.W. 174
Nicklesburg, G.W.E. 14

Oeming, M. 15
Ogden, G.S. 50f.
Ollenburger, B.C. 13, 52f.
Ong, W.J. 44

Pedersen, J. 37, 48
Perdue, L.G. 26f., 47
Porteous, N.W. 22, 98
Preuss, H.D. 13, 151

von Rad, G. 13, 40, 51f., 152, 159, 173
Reventlow, H. Graf 13
Rofé, A. 71

Rowley, H.H. 16
Rylaarsdam, J.C. 153, 176f.

Schmid, H.H. 15, 24, 151, 177
Scott, R.B.Y. 44, 105
Seybold, K. 72
Skehan, P.W. 92
Smith, M.S. 156
Stadelman, L.I.J. 54
Stoebe, H.J. 69
Stolz, F. 52

Talmon, S. 54
Terrien, S. 13
Thomas, D. Winton 16, 101
Tromp, N. 72
Turner, E. 26f.
Turner, V. 26, 52

Ullendorff, E. 108

Volten, A. 45, 174

Westermann, C. 13, 57
Whybray, R.N. 47, 100, 102, 104, 110,
   117f., 126, 145, 158, 161
Williams, J.G. 42
Williamson, H.G.M. 25, 97
Wilson, J.V. Kinnier 67
Wright, C.J.H. 141
Wiseman, D.J. 66
Würthwein, E. 21, 26

Yates, F.A. 173

Zimmerli, W. 13, 20f., 77f., 152, 160

Subject index

Abomination 60, 164, 166
Afterlife 167
Amenemope 24, 95
Amos 53
Anger 66, 73
Apocalyptic 51, 173f.
Apostasy 71
Asa 71

Babylon 17, 174
Ben Sira 119f.
Blessing 72, 130ff. 147, 162
Blood revenge 133

Canaan 40
Canon 14f., 91, 93, 178
City 110, 125, 128f.
Cleanness 53ff., 56f.
Covenant 125, 153, 157
Creation 20, 46, 56f., 86, 91f., 114,
  135, 154f., 157
Cult 47ff., 52ff., 85ff., 131, 154,
  162ff., 172, 177f.
Curse 66, 72, 85, 131, 148, 176
Cyrus 116

Daniel 173f.
David 97, 104, 111, 179
Death 49, 51, 56, 72ff., 77, 83f., 90ff.,
  176
Deuteronomy 26, 37
Disease 85ff., 120
Dispersion 28, 30, 36, 39, 57f., 64,
  13ff., 121, 124f., 129, 143, 152, 154
Dreams 174

Edomites, 17
Education 41, 107ff., 126f., 129f.,
  136ff.
Egypt 94ff., 107
Elijah 103
Elisha 71, 75, 103
Esther 116, 128
Exile 28f., 54f., 57, 59, 64, 77, 81,
  96f., 112f., 116, 124f.
Ezekiel 31, 54, 58, 78, 81

Fear of the Lord 60ff., 83f., 125, 155,
  158, 161, 163f.
Folklore 106, 111, 174
Folk wisdom 22f., 41, 110, 124, 150
Fool 171, 177
Foreigner 38
Forgiveness 89, 164

Guilt 87, 163f.

Health 65ff., 69f.
Hellenism 24, 34, 39, 42, 66, 90, 92,
  117, 120
Hezekiah 70, 86f., 105, 170
Holiness 54, 57, 59f., 66, 72f., 81, 88
Holiness Code 59
Honour 37, 144
Household 123ff.
Humility 167f.
Humour 41f.

Intention 162ff., 170ff.
Isaiah 70, 114

Jeremiah 31, 54, 58, 115f.
Jesus of Nazareth 15
Job 84ff., 120, 159
Joseph 173f.
Justice 94ff., 98ff., 101, 105f., 117ff., 133

Kingship 22ff., 41, 94ff., 96ff., 100f., 103f., 134, 179

Law 95ff.
Life 49, 51, 56, 72f., 77, 83f., 91, 147f., 176
Liminality 26ff., 30, 52, 57f., 81, 124
Literacy 43ff., 129f.

Maat 22, 40, 45
Magic 67, 74ff., 93, 98ff., 173ff.
Mashal 23, 46
Messianic Hope 113, 121
Miracle 159, 176
Monotheism 156ff.
Moses 39, 69, 93, 179
Mythology 54ff., 57, 63f., 90, 121, 155, 176

National Wisdom 46f.
Near East 40, 42, 45, 47, 56, 62, 66ff., 94ff., 108f., 124, 152
Nebuchadnezzar 116
Neighbour 38, 132ff.

Oracles 177
Order 45, 48f., 56ff., 90ff., 95f., 148f., 154f., 169
Origin of Wisdom 156

Pharmacology 66f., 69, 75, 92
Politics 94ff., 153
Poverty 103, 109, 134f., 144, 146
Prayer 125, 127, 165f., 170
Prophecy 21, 31f., 38, 54, 58, 177, 179
Prostitution 142f.
Proverbial sayings 42
Providence 117, 119, 121, 157, 159ff., 164ff., 169, 175

Qoheleth 24, 34, 38, 42, 50f., 60, 90ff., 148ff., 153, 160f., 164ff., 174f., 178

Restoration 32
Retribution 159, 164f., 167
Revelation 153, 177ff.
Rites de Passage 27
Ruth 128

Sacrifice 163f., 172
Sapiental Religion 151ff.
Satan 85f.
Scribe 129
Shame 37, 44
Sheba, Queen of 108
Sheol 74, 162
Signs 46, 169f.
Sin 68, 73ff., 88, 162ff., 172
Slavery 144
Sojourner 38
Solomon 18, 99, 104ff., 118, 121, 179
Space 52f.
Suffering 84ff.
Sumeria 17

Temple 29, 36, 52f., 58, 63f., 77f., 81, 84, 96, 106, 124, 127, 130, 137, 150, 154, 178
Ten Commandments 137
Theodicy 31, 84, 86
Theology, Old Testament 13f., 20, 36ff.
Theophany 70
Time 48f.
Torah 20, 31, 35, 37, 153, 166, 177ff.
Transcendence 164f.

Universalism 20, 38, 43, 57, 64, 97, 115ff., 154f., 158
Urim and Thummin 169f.

Vows 59f., 164

Wealth 108f., 131ff., 143f., 147, 161
Women 140ff.
Work 145ff.

Scripture references

Old Testament

Genesis
1:1–2:4a	57
1:357	
1:4	57
1:10	57
1:14	48
3:16	73
3:17–19	148
9:8–17	48
40:1–41:36	174
41:39	174

Exodus
3:17	29
15	93
15:17	52
15:22–26	69f.
19:5–6	26, 59
23:1–3	133
28:30	169
34:23	29

Leviticus
17–26	59

Deuteronomy
4:32–40	20
5–9	37
7:6	59
14:21	38
16:18–20	99
17:8–13	170

17:9	98f.
26:1–11	147
28:1–6	148
28:1–14	78
28:1–30:20	147f.
28:15–68	78
28:21	79
28:22–24	79

1 Samuel
8:10–18	112

2 Samuel
2:1	170
3:22–30	133
3:29	133
5:19	170
5:23	170
5:25	170
7:1–17	97, 112
14:27	98
16:14–23	67
18:10–11	67

1 Kings
3:3–15	105
3:9	105
3:11	105
3:16–28	99, 106
4:29–34	107
4:32–33	107
4:33	75
8:45	58
10:1–25	108

2 Kings
4:29	76
4:31	76
5:1–19	71
20:1–11	70
20:7	70

1 Chronicles
3:17–20	97

2 Chronicles
16:12	71

Job
1:15	85
1:17	85
1:19	85
2:3	87
2:4–6	85
2:7	85
12:12–25	159
19:1–22	85
38–41	56
39:13–18	56

Psalms
1	16
2	112
37	16
38	89
38:3–8	73f.
45	112
46	52
48	52
73	16, 52

89	112	10:29	160	17:25	139
90:5–6	49	11:10–11	110	18:14	80
104	16	11:12	134	19:1	161
104:12–23	148	11:29	140	19:4	134
104:19–23	50	11:30	79	19:6	134
104:24	158	12:1	138	19:7	135
104:24–26	55	12:4	142	19:12	100
104:27–28	148	12:7	160	19:17	135
110	112	12:9	146	19:18	139
119	16	12:11	145	19:21	168
132	112	12:18	80	19:23	61
		12:24	145	20:5	171
Proverbs		12:28	77	20:8	101
1–9		13:14	77	20:9	172
18, 24, 44, 61, 81, 150, 153		13:22	132	20:24	168
		13:24	139	20:25	59
1:1–9:18	17f.	14:1	131	20:26	101
1:7	83	14:11	131	20:27	171
1:8	129	14:20	134	20:30	139
1:8–9	136	14:27	60, 77	21:2	162
2:5–8	62	14:30	79	21:9	141
3:1–3	82	14:31	135	21:19	141
3:7	62	15:3	162	21:27	163
3:8	65, 82	15:5	138	21:30	176
3:11	62	15:6	131	21:31	169
3:12	62	15:8	165	22:4	61
3:16	82	15:9	162	22:6	139
3:18	82	15:11	162	22:11	134, 172
3:26	62	15:16	60, 161	22:17–24:22	18, 24
3:33	131	15:20	139	22:22–31:31	33
4:1–5	136f.	15:26	171	23:1–12	129
4:20–22	82	15:29	166	23:27	61
5:1–23	142	15:33	61	24:21	61
5–9	142f.	16:1	168	24:21–22	99
6:1–5	135	16:2	162	24:27	145
6:20–21	137	16:3	170	24:28	134
6:24	142	16:6	61, 164	24:30–34	145f.
6:26	142	16:8	161	25:1–29:27	18
7:1–27	142	16:9	167	25:1	105
7:6–27	142	16:10	98	25:2	102
8:1–23	158	16:12	103	25:7–8	135
8:1–31	114	16:12–13	98	25:9–10	135
8:1–36	142	16:14–15	100	25:17	135
8:15–16	115	16:24	80	28:5	61
8:22	158, 177	16:33	169f.	28:9	166
8:22–23	157	17:3	162	28:14	61
8:22–31	165	17:6	128	28:15	103, 117
9:10	60f., 83	17:8	176	28:16	103
9:10–12	82, 89	17:16	129	29:2	103
9:13–18	142	17:17	132	29:4	117
10–29	44, 60, 96	17:22	80	29:5	134
10–31	24	17:23	139	29:12	117
10:1–22:16	18	17:24	132	30:1–33	18

30:3 — 60
30:15–33 — 46
31 — 142
31:1–19 — 129
31:1–31 — 18
31:30 — 61

Qoheleth (Ecclesiastes)
3:2–9 — 50
3:16–22 — 90
3:21 — 176
3:22 — 90
4:1 — 161
4:4 — 149
4:5 — 149
4:6–8 — 149
4:7–8 — 150
5:1–6 — 60
5:1–7 — 164
5:2 — 165
5:12–20 — 149
6:12 — 176
7:1–8 — 34
7:1–14 — 92
7:7 — 161
8:2–4 — 117
8:4 — 167
8:10–13 — 161
8:10–11 — 167
8:12–13 — 165, 167
8:17 — 176
12:13–14 — 178

Isaiah
1:10–11 — 163
28:1–8 — 170
38:1–22 — 70
38:9–20 — 86
38:21 — 70, 74
40:13–14 — 46, 158
45:1–6 — 116
53:3–5 — 68
53:6 — 69

Jeremiah
7 — 58
7:12–15 — 116
7:21–26 — 163
7:30 — 58
8:3 — 28
16:13 — 28
17:4 — 28
29:10–14 — 58

Ezekiel
4:9–17 — 88
6:8–10 — 28
6:12 — 28
8:1–18 — 58
9 — 58
11:16 — 58, 81
12:6 — 28
13:13–23 — 76
36:25–27 — 59
40–48 — 53, 58

47:1–12 — 53
47:9 — 78
47:12 — 78

Daniel
2:12–30 — 174
9:7 — 39

Amos
5:21–24 — 163
7:17 — 54

Habakkuk
3:4–5 — 70

Old Testament Apocrypha

Sirach (Ecclesiasticus)
10:3–4 — 120
10:10 — 120
10:14 — 120
11:11–13 — 146
38:1–8 — 93

New Testament

Matthew
Matt 5:8 — 172

1 Corinthians
1 Cor. 2:6–13